GW01553082

Camera Studies of Wild Birds in their Homes

Chester Albert Reed

BIBLIOLIFE

From a painting

YOUNG BLUE JAYS

CAMERA STUDIES

—OF—

WILD BIRDS
IN THEIR HOMES

BY

CHESTER A. REED. B. S.

Author of "Land Birds," "Water Birds," "Flower Guide,"
"Nature Studies," North American Birds' Eggs," etc.

————

**With More Than 200 Illustrations From Photographs
of Living Wild Birds**

————

Chas. K. Reed,
Worcester, Mass.
1911

PREFACE

Although I had previously made many photographs in which living birds formed either the chief or a secondary object of the picture, it was in the year nineteen hundred that my first real efforts in the line of bird photography were made. The paths of camera-hunters in this line are not by any means strewn with roses. I have had my share of the necessary hard work, hardships, sometimes dangers, disappointments and the many failures to be expected. On the other hand, I have as results about two thousand good negatives and several thousand others not satisfactory to me but still passably good.

Success or failure depends practically upon the dispositions of the individual birds selected as subjects. If they are willing,—you get the picture; if not,—you pack up your outfit and depart, chalking down another failure. I have been very fortunate in this respect for "my" birds have nearly always proved very tractable; what failures I have recorded have been due chiefly to the fact that I was not willing to cause undue suffering to the little birds either from lack of food or too long exposure to hot sun-rays. I have always worked upon the principle that no bird photograph is worth even the risk of destruction to a nest of little birds. I speak of this because I wish to impress upon all my readers who may undertake bird photography that pictures must always take a place secondary to the welfare of the little birds.

A few minutes exposure to hot rays of a burning sun may prove fatal to young birds;—therefore always when possible have them shaded. Digestion, in a young bird, takes place very rapidly; an hour without food may prove fatal to a very young bird,—therefore do not be the means of causing the parents to withhold food from the little ones for long at a time. Changing the location of a nest even but a short distance may cause the owners to desert it or may leave it exposed to attacks from cats, squirrels or other enemies,—therefore do not for any reason remove a nest from its original site.

I have selected, as far as possible, pictures in series showing the various happenings at nests of the different birds. Unfortunately limited space will not permit of showing my large series of sea birds and birds of prey, so I have selected chiefly the more common song and insectivorous birds

Every half-tone shown is from a photograph of an authentic nest in its original location as chosen by the bird or of living, free, wild birds. The majority of these are of my own making, but to fill in series I have used a few that have been published in American Ornithology I wish to give credit to the makers of these as follows:

G. C. Embody, Fig 13.
C. A. Smith, Fig 105-6, 83.
A. R. Dugmore, Fig 104, 212
G. E. Moulthrope, Fig. 44-5. 50, 253.
J. H. Miller, Fig. 41, 80, 252, 254, 71. 111
J. E. Seebold, Fig. 34-5.
R. H. Beebe, Fig 114, 234, 242, 62, 67. 257, 189, 85-6
I. E Hess, Fig. 248-9, 93.
E. L. Bickford, Fig 166
J. M. Schreck, Fig. 238, 246-7
A. R. Spaid, Fig 69, 70, 130.
A. J. Meyer, Fig 199.
L. S. Horton, Fig. 97, 8
F. R Miller, Fig. 135-6, 48, 51.
N. F. Stone, Fig. 17, 53.
W. F Smith, Fig. 73, 122.
A. D. Wheedon, Fig. 250, 112

CONTENTS

INTRODUCTION.

Very few persons as they look at pictures in magazines or in books ever give an instant's thought as to the time, the patience or perhaps hardships the photographer might have endured in the making of them. With the general public, the prevalent idea is that anyone with a camera of any kind can take a "snap-shot" of anything and get a good picture. As a matter of fact, very few good pictures of any subject are ever secured by the commonly accepted "snap-shot" method. Some thought and study, even though it be done almost instantly, must be given as to the composition and the probable appearance of the finished picture.

I have done nearly all kinds of photography,—landscape, marine, portraiture, pet animals, press photography (which is very exacting). etc. I do not believe that any other class of photography offers the difficulties or has as large a percentage of failures as will be encountered by one who essays photographing living. wild birds

Some of the pictures that follow were obtained with the greatest of ease but they were of exceptional birds and I am duly thankful to them for the consideration they showed me. Others represent hours and even days of hard work and frequent disappointments. It was only by the very narrowest margin that the taking of one of the series shown did not lead to the printing of my obituary.

In the last chapter I give some details that may be of assistance to those who wish to make pictures of birds. I only speak of the difficulties here so that those who scan the pictures on the succeeding pages may not think one can grab up a camera, rush to the woods and take pictures of birds offhand. Just remember that more than seventy-five per cent. of the adult birds. whose pictures are shown, were between three and four feet from the lens of the camera and figure out how many birds you ever approached as closely as that.

BIRD STUDIES IN BLACK AND WHITE

THE CHICKADEE

We were wending our way along a narrow country lane, hedged in on either side by stone walls and bushes, when a clear "phe-be," whistled in that high-pitched, clear tone such as only the Chickadee can produce, attracted our attention. A few steps more we went, and the song suddenly ceased and changed to a series of "dee-dee-dee's" uttered

Fig. 2   NEST OF CHICKADEE

Part of stump removed to show the twelve eggs,--a very unusual number. In a birch stub, barely two feet above ground.

Fig. 3. MADAM CHICKADEE AND HER HOME.

She has a green caterpillar in her beak; as it was a lively one, she has beaten it on a branch until it is mis-shapen and nearly dead.

as rapidly as they could come from the throat of an angry bird.

It was very evident that we were uncomfortably near her home, but in which direction it was, we did not know and, had she been wise and remained silent, we probably never would have known. She came down very close to us and we saw that she had her beak filled to the brim with plant lice. How she could retain her grip upon them and still "dee-dee" so vigorously was a mystery, but the sound poured forth as rapidly from between her closed mandibles as it did later after she had deposited the food where it belonged.

Naturally, with a mother bird anxious to feed her babies, to help us, it required but a few minutes to locate the nest in a small dead tree beside the wall. Violent as had been her protestations when we first found her, she soon became quite reconciled to our presence and, in a short time, was one of the tamest birds with which I have had to deal.

For the next three or four hours we camped out right beside her home and, from the protection of a small tent, made a number of negatives of her and her mate going back and

Fig. 4. FATHER CHICKADEE AND HIS LOAD.

He was more shy than his mate and watched the tent closely each time before entering.

Chickadee

Fig. 5.   *They were lively fellows; two of them have already flown away and the one on the right is about to.*

forth. The little birds were fed, on an average, about once in every four minutes, the adults timing their visits so that one was nearly always present.

Mrs. Chickadee nearly always brought a load of tiny insects, most often plant lice,—so small that she must have brought from twenty to forty at each trip. Her mate was a philosopher, or it may have been that he was simply lazy, for he always brought single, large, white grubs, which certainly must have been easier to collect and perhaps were more filling than quantities of mites.

Fig. 6. *She was not timid and always lit on the side of the branch nearest the tent, as though to shield her little ones.*

In order to see the little Chickadees, we made the opening to the nest a little larger. We found that they were pretty large "little Chickadees" for the only difference in appearance they showed from their parents was in abbreviated tail feathers. There were six of them, five of which were very capable of short flights; in fact one slipped through my fingers and got away before I had a chance to see how large they were.

When we decided to arrange the five little fellows, that still remained, on a stick so that we might picture their parents feeding them, I knew that we would have our hands more than full; and my expectations were fully realized.

Mother Chickadee ought to have been very proud of her children, and undoubtedly she was. They obeyed every command from her, and she called "jump" (in bird language) just as often as we placed them in position to suit us. If it were possible to obtain a little knowledge of bird

Fig. 7.   A SEXTETTE OF CHICKADEES.

Try as we would we could not persuade more than six of the dozen to pose for their pictures.

language. I would give considerable to know just the sounds that mean "keep still." We finally got the pictures we wanted, but we earned them, and surely the little fellows earned the freedom that we allowed them as soon as we had made two exposures.

I have found and photographed several other families of Chickadees. one nest of which contained twelve eggs. I think this is about a record number and certainly it is more than these birds should have had. for the birch stump was so small that the eggs were arranged in tiers. They did, however. succeed in raising the entire family successfully. When the little fellows were most ready to leave home. they filled the stump from the bottom of the cavity to

Fig. 8. *Father Chickadee often made the mistake of alighting at the wrong side. It is the two little birdies at the left that are to be fed this time.*

the top. Those at the bottom were continually pushing their way up in order to get fed in their turn,—a perfect circulation of young Chickadees.

One summer, Mr. E. H. Forbush, well known in ornithological circles, wrote me that if I would appear with my

Fig. 9.   MR. FORBUSH WATCHING HIS CHICKADEE.

This bird repeatedly lit on the side, and top of the nesting box, went in and fed her little ones while Mr. Forbush was watching them through the glass front.

BLUEBIRD
From a painting

From a painting

CHIPPING SPARROW

Fig. 10. *A close view of the male bird about to enter the nesting box.*

camera he could promise me a bird treat. The next day I arrived at his house and was shown the home of a pair of Chickadees in a bird box attached to the sill of a second story shed window. It probably was the first successful attempt to induce these little birds to utilize a box attached to a dwelling.

2

Fig. 11. *They appreciate the winter lunch counter provided by bird lovers.*

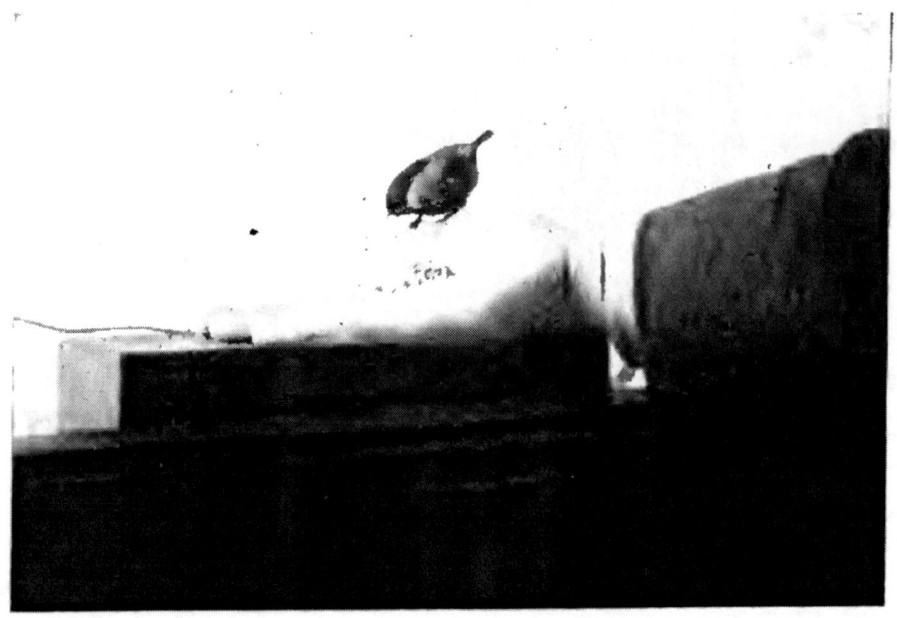

Fig. 12. *They are quite fearless in winter and occasionally feed from the hand.*

The back of the box facing the window, was removable, so that all that transpired, as the parents fed the five little birds, could be plainly watched at a distance of but two feet. The value of a family of these birds on the premises is easily seen from the fact that all shrubs and plants about the house were kept entirely free from plant lice during the season.

Fig. 13. *Cavities in orchard trees make fine nesting places.*

You will notice, by one of the accompanying pictures, that the Chickadees were not in the least afraid, but came and went even though they were being watched at close range. The little ones left the nest shortly after this picture was taken, flying first to Mr. Forbush's shoulder, then to his hat and thence out into the wide, wide world.

Chickadees can easily be induced to remain about farm houses in summer if they are occasionally fed during the winter, when food is scarce or difficult to obtain. Even if the orchard contains no trees with decayed limbs, in which they can nest, they will remain if you wire short sections of decayed birches to some of the trees.

Fig. 14. *A piece of suet is just the thing for Chickadees on cold wintry days.*

Fig. 15. *A white-breasted Nuthatch and the bountiful repast of nuts and suet provided for him by a human friend.*

Fig. 16. *Does a Nuthatch like nuts? Note the inverted position. These birds love to be head downward.*

WHITE-BREASTED NUTHATCH

Here is an acrobat worthy of notice. Apparently in defiance of all laws of gravity, he nimbly runs down tree trunks head-foremost, with never a falter. To him, the under side of a limb is just as secure a resting place as the top. A very close watch of his movements will show how he is able to get into such unbalanced positions; one foot is carried well forward under his breast but the other is reached back and grasps the bark behind so he can progress downward in a series of quick hitches.

22

Fig. 17.   THE NUTHATCH HOME
A section of the limb removed to show the interior

Most of the nuthatch nests I have found have been located in holes in large chestnut trees, from twenty to fifty feet from the ground and of course, entirely unsuited for photographic purposes. Finally a pair was located breeding in a decayed limb of an apple tree very near a farm house and only about six feet from the ground. At the bottom of the cavity, on a soft bed of grasses and feathers, lay five, delicate eggs covered with reddish brown specks.

The male was very attentive to his mate while she was sitting upon her eggs and often carried tempting grubs to her. Again he would slide down the limb just above her

Fig. 18. IN AN OLD APPLE TREE.

Fig. 19.　CLEANING THE NEST.
Note the male bird in the rear.

Fig. 20.　FATHER NUTHATCH ARRIVES.

Fig. 21. *The male Nuthatch was a handsome bird with a glossy black crown.*

and utter a soft "yank, yank" until she gave an answering "yank" from within. He did not spend much of his time in the apple tree, for to have done so would have advertised his home too conspiciously, but he was always within sight in the woods across the road. He could often be heard diligently hammering to get grubs that were concealed beneath the bark.

Fig. 22.

Fig. 23. *The little birds and their parents assumed all manner of poses.*

27

I often watched him, standing on the shaggy bark of a chestnut tree, pounding away with might and main, sometimes putting his bill under an edge of the bark and prying until it seemed as though he might snap his bill in the middle. When hammering they always take their position above their work, just as the human wood-chopper likes to do.

Fig. 24. *Caterpillars were eaten with a relish.*

The male nuthatch, known by his glossy black crown, never took a turn at sitting upon the eggs leaving such duties exclusively to his gray-crowned wife. After the eggs hatched he assumed the greater part of the burden of feeding the little ones, coming with food at least twice as often as did his mate. I suspect this was because he was more skillful at uncovering larvae and grubs, and not because of any desire on his part to work more than necessary.

Fig. 25.

Fig. 26.   *The inconvenience of being in the way when brother's turn comes.*

Fig. 27. *His children were clamoring to be fed, so loudly that, in his excitement, father stood on one of them.*

Besides grubs and larvae, the little ones were fed upon many kinds of millers and sometimes upon cracked corn that was picked up in the hen yard. Two weeks after the eggs hatched, the young were nearly large enough to leave the nest. They looked almost like their parents, the males having glossy black crowns, and the females gray ones. The five youngsters were arranged side by side on a small limb and many views taken of the parents as they fed them. Both parents never came to the branch at the same time, though one would often stay in the apple tree and watch while the other one was pushing food into the cavernous mouths. The little birds were very tractable, not behaving at all like the little chickadees. In fact they did not fly from the branch at all, but they were inclined to clamber along it so as to reach the trunk of the tree.

The name Nuthatch was given to birds of this family because of their supposed habit of hammering or "hatching" at nuts to get at the meat within, but as far as I know, none of the four species found in the United States ever open nuts of any kind. They are, however, very fond of the kernels and are often fed upon them as well as suet during winter months, by kind-hearted folks. Nuthatches, Chicka-

Fig. 28. BROTHER AND SISTER.

Note the gray crown on the female and the jet black one of the male.

dees, Downy and Hairy Woodpeckers are usually resident wherever they are found so that, besides the pleasure gained by watching them eat from the table provided for them, they may remain and nest the next summer in the vicinity. Any community that is so fortunate as to be the dwelling place of a number of these birds is to be envied, for they do inestimable good by destroying many insects that ravage shade trees, fruit trees and plants.

AIR SCOUTS.

Certain long-winged birds spend a large proportion of their existence a-wing, dashing across the fields, swooping across ponds, skimming over housetops, even sweeping the clouds. These birds may very fittingly be termed "air-scouts,"—always on the lookout for insect enemies. They are constantly on duty scouring the skies, performing for mankind, in times of peace, services incomparably greater than those expected of our aeroplane scouts in time of war.

Chimney Swift

One of the most useful of these scouts is a "city dweller."
Chimney Swifts at one time nested only in hollow trees and in caves or crevices in cliffs. To-day for some unaccountable reason they nest almost exclusively within the depths of unused chimneys. We can readily understand why they like to live in cities for there the little gnats and flies they like so well are the most abundant, but it is not so plain why any species of bird should desert the comparatively clean cavities of decayed trees for the dirty, sooty interiors of brick chimneys. It seems like a retrogressive rather than a progressive development.

Swifts return to the northern states about the middle of April each year, but they delay their nest building until early May when the weather is more settled. It is quite necessary that the air be dry when they make their homes for they are held together entirely by glue which does not harden rapidly in damp weather. This glue is made by the swifts from their saliva; it is very hard and almost waterproof when dry.

Their nest building is very interesting to watch but it is a slow operation often keeping the two birds busy for a week more. It is made of twigs varying in length from half an inch to a couple inches. They must of necessity be dead twigs for the birds break them from the tips of branches,

Fig. 29. CHIMNEY SWIFT.

Note how the tail spines assist them in clinging to the upright surface.

while hovering in the air; I have on numerous occasions seen them secure nesting material in this way but never, except twice, did I see them alight on the ground to pick up pieces.

The inside of the chimney, at the point selected, is smeared with glutinous saliva and the little twig covered with the same; each tiny stick is added in this manner until the nest projects from the wall for two or three inches and the interior is an inch deep. It makes a very strong little home when properly made. Often, however, they fail to make the front wall sufficiently high so that some of the eggs roll or are pushed out by the sitting bird.

The eggs, white and from three to five in number, require incubating for nearly three weeks before they hatch. The young birds remain in the chimney for nearly a month longer before they are able to venture out on their wings. So the nesting of swifts is a slow process requiring about two months, while the ordinary insectivorous bird will get its little ones out of the nest sometimes within a month from the time the foundation was first commenced.

Long before the little swifts are able to fly they get exercise by climbing about the inside of their chimney-home. A pair of swifts always built their nest directly opposite the stove-pipe opening in the chimney of an old country house. I have often removed the cap to look at the eggs or, later, to see the four little swifts clinging to the chimney directly under the nest. They are nimble little things and seldom lose their hold. Sometimes they do, and fall to the bottom of the chimney but, by the aid of the wings, their sharp·little claws and their spiney tails, they can climb to the nest again. If you have examined Chimney Swifts closely, you probably have noticed that the shafts of the tail feathers project beyond the webs making sharp little spines that are of great assistance to the birds in their manner of living.

As it is obviously impossible for a bird to fly upwards in

a vertical line and the narrow confines of a chimney would seem to make such flight a necessity, I often used to wonder just how the adult birds left the home. Of course a boy's curiosity has to be satisfied so one day I removed the board from the front of the old-fashioned fireplace, concealed

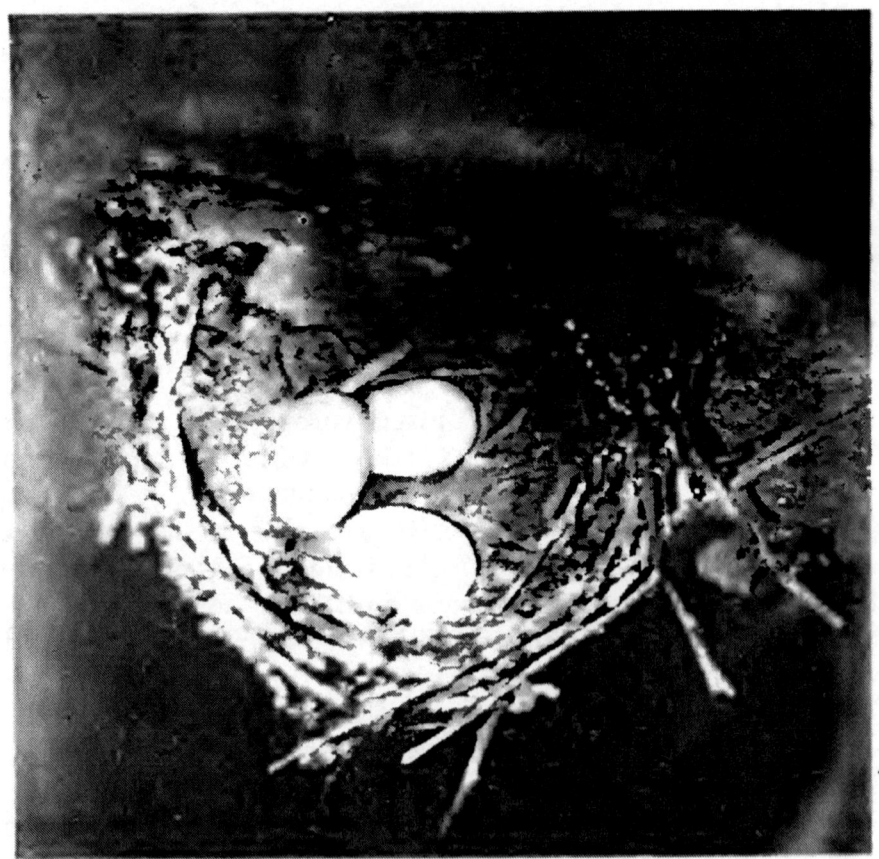

Fig. 30. NEST OF CHIMNEY SWIFT.

Taken by reflected light from a mirror.

myself within and watched until my quest for knowledge was satisfied. Their movements were so rapid and the loosened soot would persist in getting in my eyes so much that my research was no easy one.

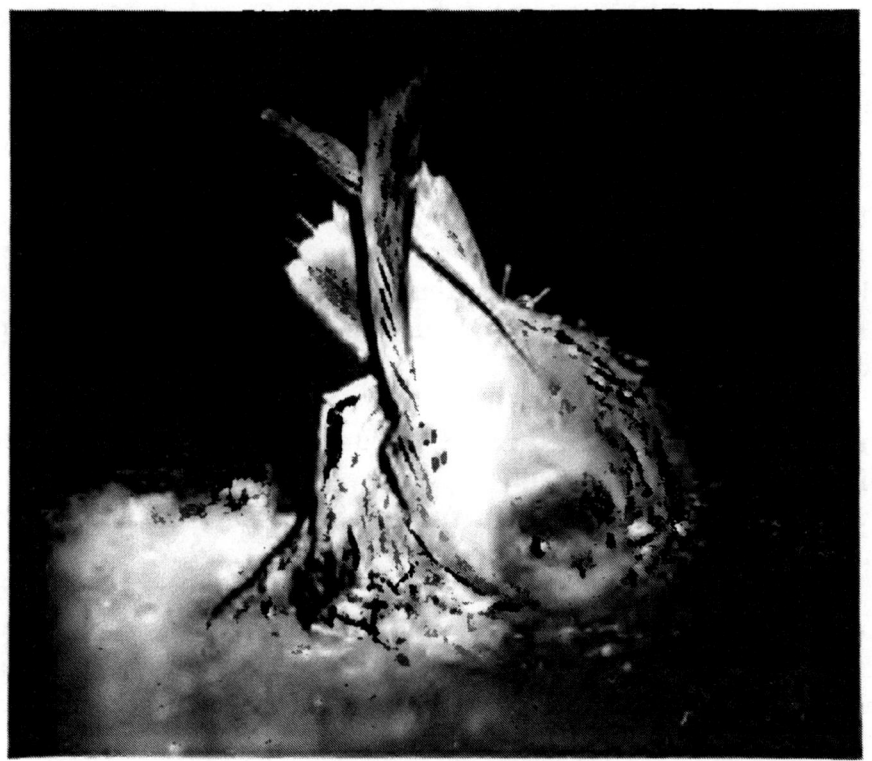

Fig. 31.　CHIMNEY SWIFT ON NEST.

A little blurred because the bird jumped when the light was flashed on her.

The chimney was about eighteen inches in width. Starting from the nest, the bird would leap upward, and two strong flaps of the narrow wings would carry him to the opposite wall a little more than a foot above where he started; he just barely touched the side, whirled and two more beats raised him another foot. He only had about fifteen feet to rise before reaching the top and it only took about ten of the rapid side-to-side flights to accomplish it.

The return to the nest was more difficult to watch as the birds came dashing down with the speed of a bullet, apparently not touching the sides at all. Almost before I could see them coming they would have turned and be clinging beside the nest.

The rapid twittering of Chimney Swifts is often heard as they wheel about overhead, and the sound is greatly augmented when a little swift is about to make his maiden flight into the unknown. All the adults and young in the vicinity gather to celebrate the event and to encourage the little fellow in his attempt. The young swifts get their wings strongly developed before leaving the chimney by flights from side to side, so that they have little to fear as they emerge into the open and follow the others over the house tops.

Swifts are used by many as weather prophets and their prognostications seem to come true far more often than those of our government experts. When swifts fly high, fair weather is presumed to follow; when they fly low, look out for rain. Whether they fly high or fly low, however, you may be quite certain that it is not the state of the weather that influences them but means that the food they seek is most abundant at that level. The weather may or may not influence the altitudes at which the winged insects happen to be.

Nighthawks and Whip-poor-wills

These two birds, often confused with one another by many, are similar in form but distinctive in plumage and very different in habits. I will first note some of the distinctions.

Nighthawk has a white throat, white bar across the outer wing feathers, white bar across the middle of the outer tail feathers and the tail a trifle forked (female has the throat and tail bars rather buffy-colored). Whip-poor-will has a black throat, no white on wings, rounded tail and white tips to the outer feathers. These differences in plumage are positive and should distinguish the two whether seen flying or perching. But there are other differences.

37

Fig. 32.   NIGHTHAWK.

Sitting upon her eggs on the gravel roof of a city block.

Nighthawks fly most at dusk or on cloudy days, frequenting open localities or cities; thousands see them every day during the season they are with us. Whip-poor-wills are night birds, frequenting woods and are seen by but comparatively few persons. The call of the Nighthawk is a rasp-

Fig. 33. *The male spend daytime sitting lengthwise along limbs and is quite difficult to see.*

ing, nasal "peenk," given while flying; that of the Whip-poor-will is a loudly and rapidly whistled "whip-poor-will" often repeated twenty or more times in succession; this song is uttered while perched in the tops of trees.

The differences between the two birds are so great that there is really little reason for confusion, whenever or wherever they are seen or heard. ..

Nighthawks are past masters in the art of aviation. There are no feats of skill performed by other birds that cannot be equalled by these. During June and July they can

Fig. 34. NEST AND EGGS OF NIGHTHAWK.

The eggs are laid on the bare surface of a flat stone.

usually be seen and heard in great numbers about any large city as they circle high in the air or sweep in graceful curves over the tops of the buildings. In the country they frequent the edges of woods or burned areas where flying insects are the most easily secured. They are very sociable birds and often hunt in large flocks. I have watched fully a hundred of them at a time as they swept back and forth across a large field, curving, skimming and cavorting about in a perfect maze; with never a falter they crossed and re-crossed paths, each seeming to read the other's mind perfectly so that imminent collisions were always averted.

Nighthawk bills are very small but the mouth opens to a point below the eyes so that the gape is enormous. Their food is entirely caught while on the wing,—either by snapping up individual moths or beetles or by dashing through swarms of gnats, with wide-open mouths gathering them in by the hundreds.

During the mating season the males often perform wonderful evolutions in the air. Sometimes they make perpendicular descents from high altitudes shooting downwards with folded wings at bullet-like speed and turning upward so suddenly that the air rushing through their wings produces a hollow "booming." On a warm, still evening during early June and the latter part of May, these "boomings" may very frequently be heard.

Although so exceedingly expert in aerial evolutions, Nighthawks are very awkward when on the ground. Their small, weak feet give them a very wobbly gait so that they often require the services of their wings to keep their balance. When roosting on the limbs of trees and fence rails they almost invariably sit lengthwise, their mottled plumage and motionless attitudes rendering them very inconspicuous.

They build no nest at all,—just lay their two mottled eggs on the bare ground, usually choosing a small sandy spot in a pasture or in very open woods; frequently they are laid in hollows on rocks or even (very commonly) on

Fig. 35. NIGHTHAWK ON ITS NEST.

Note that it is not at all conspicuous, Sometimes they can be touched before they will fly.

flat gravel roofs of city blocks. The eggs resemble the pebbles so closely that it is difficult to see them. A friend knowing that I am always ready to go almost anywhere to secure a good bird picture, came and informed me that a Nighthawk was sleeping on his roof every day, that it sat behind a certain chimney and would allow him to approach within a few feet before flying. I thought it strange that he made no mention of seeing the eggs, but I went along and, sure enough, the bird, a female Nighthawk, was just where he said it would be. When we were about four feet distant it sailed easily away over the surrounding roofs. My friend watched the bird until it disappeared and then turned to me with a self-satisfied air saying: "I knew it would be here; strange that it comes to the same building to roost every day, isn't it?" He could hardly believe his eyes when I showed him the two eggs the bird had been covering. He had started this bird off at least half a dozen times and had not noticed them.

If the bird is flushed from the eggs when incubation is well advanced, she will attempt to lead the intruder away by feigning lameness,—a very easy matter for a Nighthawk as they progress very awkwardly on the ground anyway. Young Nighthawks are first covered with fine down but, unlike most birds that are so clothed, they move about indifferently on their feet. One or the other of the parents sits beside them during the day and they are not fed until between dusk and daylight.

Whip-poor-will

Unless disturbed, Whip-poor-wills pass the whole day dozing on horizontal limbs or upon fallen tree trunks. They are even more averse to moving during daylight than Owls. As soon, however, as the mantle of night has fallen over the woods, they become very active, swooping close to the ground to gather up luckless beetles or dashing upward to capture passing moths. Their bills are small but their

Fig. 36.   NEST AND EGGS OF WHIP-POOR-WILL.

The eggs are laid on the ground or leaves with no semblance of a nest.

Fig. 37. WHIP-POOR-WILL AND YOUNG

Color protection is so perfect that even the lens could hardly distinguish the bird.

mouths are perhaps even larger than those of Nighthawks. They swallow, with ease, the largest of the moths and sphinges and relish equally well small gnats or winged ants. Chuck-wills-widows, larger members of the same genus, found commonly in the Southern States are even more voracious and devour anything that happens to be a-wing at night and that will go in their enormous mouths; frequently

Fig. 38. WHIP-POOR-WILL.

Notice how perfectly she blends into the surrounding leaves. The living bird as seen by the eye shows no plainer than it does here.

the remains of small birds are found in their stomachs, probably caught while flying from one perch to another.

Whip-poor-wills are very noisy on warm, clear, still nights. One night I pitched my tent beside a juniper tree on a point of land making out into a beautiful lake. This particular tree happened to be the favorite lookout perch of a Whip-poor-will, or else he was attarcted to it by the

white tent. At any rate one of them sat in the top of this
little juniper from nine o'clock until one. It seemed to me
that he "whipped-poor-will" constantly all this time. The
notes are not objectionable and are interesting to listen to
for a few minutes at a time, but four hours of continuous
performance was too much for me, especially as the performer was within twenty feet. I went out and gathered
a few stones; as the first one went by he evidently though
it some species of moth for he darted after it the same as

Fig 39. TREE SWALLOW.

These swallows nest in hollow trees or in bird boxes.

bats do if anything is thrown up in front of them, and
then returned to the tree top and "whip-poor-willed" again.
The next stone crashed through the tree below him and I
saw his shadowy form flit overhead across the lake where
his calls soon mingled with others of his kind and I was
left undisturbed by them for the balance of the night.

Fig. 40. NEST AND EGGS OF BANK SWALLOW.
Bank sliced away to show nest and length of tunnel.

The Whip-poor-will makes no nest but lays its two faintly mottled eggs on dead leaves on the ground in woods, usually where they will be partly concealed by overhanging brush. During daylight they trust to their protective coloration entirely and it rarely fails them. You can readily judge from the photographs shown how closely they harmonize in color and markings with their surroundings. If one knows the location of a nest and uses due caution in approaching he can nearly always touch them before they will leave.

The feathers of all birds of this genus are exceedingly soft so that their flight is entirely noiseless. At night they can thread their way in and out through the branches with an ease and grace that is incredible. I believe their sight too, at night, is even keener that that of any of the owls.

SWALLOWS

Swallows are the most active, most persistant and most graceful gleaners of the atmosphere. Of the six species found in the eastern states, all except the Bank and the

Fig. 41. YOUNG BANK SWALLOWS.

Rough-winged Swallows have taken up their abodes in buildings built by man. Even the Bank Swallow commonly nests in holes in banks where men are constantly at work digging; and the Rough-winged species often makes its homes among the stones of bridge foundations. Barn Swallows nest within our barns. Eave or Cliff Swallows make their homes under the eaves. Tree Swallows live in little bird houses nailed to the sides of buildings or holes in our orchard trees and Purple Martins live in colonies, often in very large, elaborate, many-roomed houses topping poles set on lawns. No other class of birds has become so almost-domesticated as the swallows

Swallows are always sociable: they sometimes nest in very large colonies and always in as large numbers as the locality will support or furnish sites for. Of course it is more difficult for Tree Swallows to find a sufficient number of suitable cavities for many to nest near together, but I have found a half dozen pairs of these nesting in one orchard.

The illustration in which part of the bank has been cut away gives a perfect idea of the nesting of Bank Swallows. The little tunnel goes horizontally in for about two feet and is then enlarged to make room for the feather-lined, grass nest. The four or five eggs are pure white without markings.

Fig. 42. A FAVORITE BRIDGE.
For many years Phoebes have nested under this old bridge.
Note the bird on the branch at left.

BIRD MASONS.

Certain of our wild birds are quite expert at handling, and use quantities of mud in the formation of the cradles for their eggs and young. Three good examples of such birds are given in this chapter. The Robin and the Wood Thrush, the home lives of which are given in another chapter, also use much mud for the foundations of their nests.

PHOEBE

Early each spring, soon after the arrival, in New England, of Bluebirds, Robins and Song Sparrows, friend Phoebe puts in his appearance,—a welcome appearance because it means that very soon a vast, kaleidoscopic procession of birds will come trooping from the south.

Phoebe is very often known as the "Bridge-Bird," not the kind of "bridge" with which so many people of this day are familiar, but the good, old-fashioned bridge that spans a stream or gully. Such a bridge, with large logs for stringers and planks for a surface, crosses a little brook along which I like to wander. Each year, for as long a time as any living person can remember, Phoebes have nested under this. Of course, new nests are built each season, but they have usually been in the same spot,—above a slight projection on the side of one of the logs. The nest is gradually built up of pellets of mud, held together with grasses and mosses. Sometimes the outside is almost wholly of green moss, giving a most beautiful effect. The inside of the structure may be lined either with grass or feathers. The four or five eggs are a clear, creamy white usually with no markings, although sometimes very faint specks will show on the large end.

Besides under bridges, Phoebes make their nests in niches in cliffs, under sheds and barns, under overhanging banks, among the stones of old cellar walls, in fact any-

Fig. 43. NEST OF PHOEBE.
This nest is under the bridge shown in Fig. 42.

where so that the nest will be shaded and protected from sight and the weather

Because of the comparative darkness of the situations they choose, in which to build their homes, it is quite difficult to make satisfactory pictures of Phoebes feeding their young. Not only that, but the birds are so active that it is difficult to show the feeding process even though the light were good. Usually, reflected sunlight from a large mirror has to be used to secure illumination sufficient to make an instantaneous exposure. A picture of a Phoebe sitting upon its nest in a shed is shown, taken in this manner; also a picture of the eggs in the nest, taken by having another mirror inverted above the nest.

When a suburban trolley line crossed a certain brook, they put in very heavy iron girders for the foundation. A pair of Phoebes took a liking to this spot and built their moss-covered house on the lower flange of one girder. Here they laid their eggs and reared the family. Cars passed every thirty minutes, or as regularly as street cars usually go to such a schedule, on rails but two feet above the head of the mother as she sat upon the nest. The bird must have been entirely devoid of nerves for she never moved as the cars rumbled overhead with a clatter and roar that sounded fearful from underneath. I spent several hours under there and I was very glad to leave at the end of that time. A mirror situated on the bank below the bridge was used to throw a spot of light on the nest. The camera was set on a tripod in the water, which was only about six inches deep, while I had to crouch on a few small stones and try to keep my balance. Some cloth, tacked to the planking above and draping down to the water screened the camera and myself from the birds. From time to time, I had to push the mirror slightly so as to keep the little spot of sunlight where it would cover the nest. It was a very easy matter to secure pictures of the mother as she stood on the edge

Fig. 44. PHOEBE ON NEST.

This nest is on a beam in a shed. Sun was thrown on it by a large mirror.

55

Fig. 45. NEST AND EGGS OF PHOEBE.

This is the same nest shown in Fig. 44. Two mirrors were used,—one to reflect sunlight and the other above the nest to show the eggs.

Fig. 46.   PHOEBE AND HER FAMILY.

Taken just after feeding, by reflected sunlight.   The actual feeding was always done while the bird was hovering and was too rapid to be photographed in 1-100 of a second.

of the nest looking at the extraordinary light that shone from the bank, but I was not able to get a satisfactory picture of her actually feeding the little ones. In fact, most of the time, she would hover over the nest and feed them while a-wing, then drop to the edge and watch either the lens or the light.

Fig. 47. *This Phoebe nest was in an old cellar hole.*

58

Fig. 48.   A PAIR OF BARN SWALLOWS.

Fig. 49. NEST AND EGGS OF BARN SWALLOW.

Always lined with soft feathers.

The male bird did not come to the nest at all, while I was there. but he encouraged his mate to do so for he would stand outside. flirt his tail and utter many a harsh "phoe-be" as she was going under the bridge; he also often gave a rather pretty trill as she came out, just as though he were praising her for her bravery in going where he dared not. Most of the food brought to the nest was small moths that were caught flying over or about the edges of the brook.

BARN SWALLOW

Just as the Phoebe is the "Bridge-bird," so this is a bird of the barn. Before the advent of civilized man, they dwelt in caves or in hollow trees. So wholly have they now adapted themselves to man's ways that I have never seen, nor have I heard of an instance for many years, of one of their nests except in a building constructed by human hands.

Fig. 50.   NEST OF BARN SWALLOW.

Taken by reflected sunlight, and a second mirror above the nest to show the eggs.

Fig. 51. A DOUBLE NEST.

Note that these nests are placed on a mowing machine knife. It is well to provide projections in suitable places for these birds to build upon.

Barn Swallows make their nests or pellets of mud held together with bits of straw; bit by bit, these are attached to the side of a beam until the half-bowl-shaped structure is complete; the inside is always very warmly lined with soft feathers from barnyard fowls. Sometimes these nests are plastered to beams that are fairly smooth, and in such cases are very apt to be loosened and fall. Usually a very rough beam or a spot where there is a splinter or a nail projecting, is chosen. One of our pictures shows a nest that is built on the cutter of a mowing machine, this having been laid across two nails. Many farmers, realizing the value of these birds about their places, nail small bits of board to the bottom of some of the beams, so as to give their little friends a firm foundation for their homes.

Time after time, I have hidden in a hay mow just to watch these exceedingly graceful creatures as they skimmed in through the barn door, swept upward and landed, light as feathers, on the edge of their nests. Always, as they glided through the door, I would hear their musical twitter;

Fig. 52. YOUNG BARN SWALLOWS.

All from one nest but probably belonging to two pairs of swallows.

the little birds, waiting in the nest were listening intently for that same twitter and were always all standing up with wings fluttering and mouths wide open ready to greet their parent when he or she arrived. Each parent usually brought enough every trip to go the rounds of the hungry mouths. The food was composed almost wholly of gnats and other tiny insects that can be caught in great quantities as the swallows go swooping across the fields or over ponds.

How I longed to be able to reproduce, with the camera, the beautiful scenes that I have witnessed many times at Barn Swallow nests, but, unfortunately, they have always been in locations where the light did not allow of instantaneous pictures and always where I have been unable to use a mirror to reflect light. Their movements, as they thrust food in turn down the waiting throats are so very rapid that no exposure longer than one one hundredth of a second would secure any result except a blur.

Cliff Swallow

While the Barn Swallows usually have their homes within barns, Cliff Swallows almost as frequently fasten theirs to the outsides of such structures, on which account they are very generally known as "Eave Swallows." These Swallows are more gregarious than Barn Swallows; even in the East, where they build under the eaves of buildings, they nest in colonies varying from two or three nests to sometimes as many as fifty on one building. In the West where they have not so fully learned the ways of civilization, they nest in colonies of thousands, attaching their homes to the faces of cliffs.

Their nests are constructed in the same manner as those of Barn Swallows but are of a much different shape. The typical Cliff Swallow nest is flask-shaped; it is attached to the building or cliff by one side of the rounded bottom, which is slightly flattened, and the entrance is through an opening in the short neck that protrudes from the upper side; again the nest may have no neck but simply a round hole in the upper part of the mud dome. The outside has a very granular appearance caused by the large pellets of mud that are plastered on it. The inside is, of course, lined with feathers or grasses.

Many persons confuse this bird and the latter one, but they are very different and easily recognized. This species has no swallow or forked tail and has a light patch on the

rump and one on the forehead, both of which are very easily
seen even during flight.

Although I have seen and know of a great many of their
nesting sights my photographic experiences with these birds
are limited to one attempt. The nests were under the eaves
of a large barn, fully thirty feet above ground; time and
conditions forced me to hold the graflex camera out of a
tiny window and make exposures in a most awkward attitude. The eggs of this species are precisely like those of
the Barn Swallow,—creamy white, profusely spotted with
reddish-brown. The nests are most commonly located on
buildings near water; I have found them very commonly
plastered to the sides of ice houses.

Fig. 53.   LEAST FLYCATCHER.

Brooding her little ones.

EXPERT FLYCATCHERS.

Chebec or Least Flycatcher

The pair of Least Flycatchers, with which this chapter deals, built their nest, as may be very plainly seen in the photographs, in an apple tree. This tree was located within twenty feet of the house of a friend of mine and also of the birds.

We saw the very foundation built, in fact we noticed them carrying almost the first materials that entered into

Fig. 54. *The nest was daintly set among a cluster of green apples.*

it. The building of the home occupied the two of them for three days. They did not work very steadily for there were a great many flies and moths to be caught. The male had a favorite lookout perch at the very apex of a pear tree; he would often sit there for an hour at a time singing his

5

simple and homely song,—just a sharp, snappy "che-bec," accompanying each syllable with a quick jerk of his head.

It was a finely made nest, very firmly quilted together, of gray plant fibres, string, horsehair and fine grass, bound very tightly to its supporting twigs. A week after the nest was completed, it contained three, creamy-colored eggs; she laid no more but immediately commenced sitting, hour

Fig. 55. *Many millers, as well as other insects, were fed to the young Chebecs.*

after hour and day after day. Sometimes she did not even leave at dinner time for her mate was very thoughtful and often brought her moths and various kinds of flies. At other times he would start from his lookout perch and fly over her, with that fluttering flight that flycatchers so often affect, just to assure himself that everything went well in his home; at such times he usually uttered the beautiful little trill that these flycatchers often make when they are pleased with themselves or their surroundings.

In due course of time the eggs hatched. When the young were ten days old we made our first photographs. The nest

Fig. 56. *The food was quickly thrust far down the throat of the hungry bird-baby.*

was about ten feet from the ground, but we pulled the limb down and tied it so that their home was only eight feet up. We then backed a large covered wagon up close to the nest and from within made quite a series of pictures. The little mother was brooding the young as we backed the wagon up and, although so large an object coming so close must have frightened her, she stayed "aboard" the nest until we climbed into the wagon and began setting up the cameras within three feet of her.

We soon had everything concealed, except the lenses, by large blankets, and the little mother bird paid no more attention to us. The nest was in an exposed position, where the sun shone brightly on it during the forenoon, so she brooded the little birds a great deal. She would stand over them with wings slightly spread, warding off the fierce rays of the sun from her offspring; such was her devotion. About every five minutes her mate would bring some kind

Fig. 57. *When we placed the little birds on a branch, mother Chebec at once fed them and then looked long at the glass "eye" staring at her.*

of a winged insect for the little ones, and she would instantly dart down into the coolness of the foliage below, only to return in a few minutes to take up her task.

This pair of birds and the three young remained about the orchard until the end of summer; the next year a pair, and I think it was the same, had a nest within a few feet of where the other was, but this time it was placed where the sun did not shine on it at all; had she remembered the suffering of the previous year?

Fig. 58. *Father Chebec was in such a hurry that he trod all over one of the little birds while feeding the other.*

A Family of Redstarts

The morning of one June day found me threading my way along a narrow footpath that wound its way in and out through one of the most delightful pieces of woodland that ever echoed a bird song. As I walked slowly along, I was separating, by their voices, the many varieties of birds whose babble filled the woodland with melody.

A gleam of orange and black among the foliage, proclaims the presence of a Redstart, that alert member of the warbler family whose habits are so like those of some of the flycatchers. He was in the act of tearing fragments from a caterpillar nest; this material he carried across the path to a small maple about twenty feet from me and wound it about the framework of a nest that he and his mate had just commenced. While he was so engaged, his partner appeared with a load of plant fibres which she carefully and skilfully weaved into the growing home.

Fig. 59.   MALE REDSTART AND FAMILY

He was perfectly fearless and came as regularly as though we were not present.

Seating myself under the shade of a bush not more than ten feet away I enjoyed a two hour lesson in the art of nest-building. The male was an unusually bright-colored bird; he was very proud and conceited too. His mate was also very beautiful, even though less gaily clad than he. Undoubtedly she knew more about correct house building than Mr. Redstart, but he did not think so, and whenever she objected to his manner of doing the work, he promptly drove her away with playful snappings of his bill. In the end, she had her way as is usual in such differences, for when he went off for more material she would do his work over to suit herself.

They were exceedingly active in all their movements, their actions as they chased one another about being bewildering. Naturally, with so much play, the nest grew but slowly, and it was over a week from the time the foundation was laid before the trim little structure was completed. A week later, four possibilities of future Redstarts occupied the nest. As there were many squirrels about and the woods were often frequented by boys, I concluded it well to at least get one photographic record of the nest in case anything should happen to it. It was located only about four feet above ground and I had not the least difficulty in getting a good likeness of the female as she descended to the eggs.

The male bird, at this time was literally "out of a job," for I never saw him assist her in the duties of incubation and only once while I was present did he bring her anything to eat. He spent his time in the tops of the trees, singing, dashing after insects and driving away birds that came too near him. With the advent of the young, came an end to his period of loafing and he did his duty manfully and with much enthusiasm.

The actions of the two birds, in the presence of the camera, were quite different. The male showed a disdain for

Fig. 60. FEMALE REDSTART.

it that was amusing. I had arrived during his absence and had my head under the cloth focussing on the nest when I felt a little rush of air, a streak of orange flashed across the ground glass screen and the male was bending over his children.   How I longed to reproduce the picture that showed on the screen as he fed each of his little ones in turn, his wings quivering in his enthusiasm and his tail opening and closing like a fan. The pictures were not

Fig. 61.   BROODING THE LITTLE ONES.

made from the tent, I being concealed in a bush about ten
feet away and making exposures by means of a long tube
to release the shutter.   Several times he lit upon the camera
and once he swung upon the long rubber tube for several
seconds.   I made quite a number of pictures of him but
many were failures because of the rapidity of his movements.   His mate was much more cautious in her manner
of approach, in fact she seemed to fear the camera more
than she had when I made her picture before, but after she
became acquainted with me she was very tame.   The quar-
tet of youngsters were very bright.   When they were a week
old, their curiosity was fully developed.   They had just the
faintest suspicion of feathers on them, their almost bald
heads looking very comical as they hung them over
the edge of the nest and watched their parents foraging.

74

They were naughty too, at times, as is shown by the picture
of the mother trying to brood them. She turned and
twisted and poked at them in her endeavors to keep them
under her, but they would insist on sticking their heads out
to see what was going on. The one on the right really looks
as though he were laughing at her vain attempts to control
him.

The nest, which was plenty large enough for the eggs
and for the little birds in their first stages, is shown by the
pictures of the male feeding them, to be entirely too small
to accomodate them as they get larger. We cannot but pity
the poor little fellow that is vainly trying to push his way
up, but we may rest assured that when it comes his turn to
be fed, he will not be forgotten. At no time, while I was
watching them, did they feed the little birds upon large
insects such as many of the smaller birds frequently do.
All food brought seemed to be small winged insects or little
caterpillars that they picked up from the ground.

Fig. 62. *A pair of Bluebirds on the top of their nesting post.*

BLUE SKIES AND BLUE BIRDS.

THE BLUEBIRD

A sweet melodious warble, a flash of the brightest of blue and there upon the decayed end of an apple bough, sits one of our very best of friends, the Bluebird. As we watch, he disappears within the opening,—surely fortune smiles upon us, for the nest hole is barely above the head,— an ideal place for using the camera.

True, the nest is on the north side of the tree and consequently in rather a dark place, but we are prepared for such emergencies and in a few minutes, the reflection from a

Fig. 63. BLUEBIRD AT ITS NEST-HOLE.

Fig. 64. A BLUEBIRD PORTRAIT.

Illuminated by reflected sunlight from a large mirror. This nest was on the north side of the tree in shadow so that without the mirror pictures could not have been secured.

large mirror makes the place as light as though it were in the bright sunlight.

We soon have the camera in readiness and retire to a place of concealment behind the next tree, holding a long black linen thread the other end of which is attached to a little device to spring the shutter. As the male bird flits to and fro in the sunlight, his blue coat is dazzling in its bril-

Fig. 65.   YOUNG BLUEBIRDS.

liancy. His sombre colored but equally melodious mate is very anxious to examine her household but evidently is afraid the square box in front of her door is some sort of a trap. She makes a great many false starts but each successive move brings her a little nearer to the goal until at last she gathers all her courage and alights on the nesting hole.

Fig. 66. IN THE DOORWAY.

Fig. 67. MOTHER BLUEBIRD AND HER YOUNG

Fig. 68. *Bluebirds like bird boxes if the English sparrows are kept away.*

Instantly a dazed expression comes over her. Something is wrong. She looks long and steadily at the dazzling reflection coming from down in the grass, then peeks around the limb at the sun that is still doing duty in its proper place. The problem proved too great for her or else she lacked the time to study over it longer, for she dived down to her nest to see how her little ones were faring.

A certain twig on a dead limb of the next tree, was a

Fig. 69. AN UNUSUAL SIGHT.

These Bluebirds nested in one arm of this scare-crow.

favorite perch for her. It allowed her a clear view of the
ground for thirty feet about; often she would drop into the
grass and capture grasshoppers or caterpillars and bear
them off to the nest. The male bird, because of fear, absolutely refused to have his portrait made. He often brought
morsels of food and gave them to his mate to carry to the

little ones,—rather ungallant of Mr. Bluebird to thus expose his mate to fancied dangers he dare not face.

Another pair of Bluebirds has nested annually, for years, in the top of a certain fence post. This same nest has, on several occasions, furnished a little joke at the expense of some of my friends. As we approached the field in which this post was located, I would casually remark that I had a little Bluebird-friend that would allow me to

Fig. 70. *The sleeve of scare-crow opened so as to show the nest and eggs.*

put my arm about her without any attempt to get away. Naturally such a statement would be viewed with some doubt and I would be called upon for proof. The proof was easy, for I had but to step up to the post and put my arm about it, the bird at the time being sitting closely upon the eggs within. Usually two broods a year were reared in this secure home.

Little bluebirds have blue backs and brownish breasts, like their parents but, like all members of the thrush family to which Bluebirds belong, they have spotted breasts and more or less spotting on their backs. This plumage is lost at the first moult and they become just like their parents.

Bluebirds do not always nest in hollow trees or fences;

Fig. 71. BLUEBIRD.

many a boy or girl has a little bird box built expressly for their use, and they are very glad to use them if English sparrows can be kept from pestering them. They also sometimes build in very odd places as can be seen by the photographs of the nest in the sleeve of a scarecrow.

BLUE JAY

Blue Jays always seem like old friends to me. I have seen a great many of them under all conditions of life. I

Fig. 72. NEST AND EGGS OF BLUE JAY.

The Blue Jay usually nests in pine trees.

have watched them through field glasses; I have looked at them over the sights of a gun; I have watched them on the ground glass of a camera; and I have kept them and watched them in captivity.

One morning, about the middle of May, two men might have been seen going along a certain pine-covered hillside. Their actions were peculiar for they stopped and looked sharply into each tree as they passed. It was very promising ground for Blue Jay nests and, to tell the truth, that is just what these men were looking for.

A bird slipped quietly out of the far side of one of the pines, but the sharp eyes of my companion caught sight of

84

Fig. 73. BLUE JAY BROODING HER YOUNG.

the flash of blue and he exclaimed, "Here it is!" About
six feet from the ground was quite a large nest built of
black twigs and rootlets, and in it were five, greenish-gray
eggs covered with darker spots. Not a sound came from
the bird that had so silently disappeared. Jays are not
birds to needlessly advertise their homes when there is the
possibility that they may escape notice.

Two days later the eggs had hatched and by Memorial
Day the little Jays were ready to leave their nest. After

Fig. 74. DINNER TIME.

having posed for their pictures they were released, except
one that went home with us where he stayed for the three
following years. A few of this bird's deeds and misdeeds

Fig. 75.   *Young Jays in Nest.*

may serve to interest and give an insight into the true nature
of all jays.

Who first gave this bird a name and why it was given, nobody knows, but almost from the first day it was known as
Kitty. Part of a room was screened off, including a large
window, for the exclusive use of Kitty, and several small
trees and a little pine were introduced so as to allow for
exercise. The first two weeks, Kitty had to be fed very
often; when anyone was in the room, she would hop about
after them with wide-open mouth and fluttering wings, always begging for more. Bread and milk, eggs and bits of

Fig. 76. *The Jays become too large for their home and are
crowded out on the neighboring branches.*

raw meat seemed perfectly satisfactory to her if they came
in large enough doses and at frequent intervals. It was
about three weeks before Kitty could fly strongly and then
her mischievousness began to assert itself at every opportunity.

Kitty seldom made typical jay calls or whistles but she

had a very great many notes of her own and would sometimes whistle and warble continuously for an hour at a time,
at times striking combinations of notes that sounded very
pretty   Wild jays, especially in Spring, often talk among
themselves with low whistles, with an effect very similar to
Kitty's song.   She never used the loud, harsh, jay scream
unless angered or greatly excited; if a dog came into the
room. she was a typical, wild jay and would raise her crest
and scream at the top of her voice   She had two whistles

Fig 77   *The day after leaving home*

that were used to denote gratification, usually when she had
played a joke on some one; always. when giving these she
would bob up and down on her legs in the most ludicrous
manner
　Many a ball player might have taken lessons, to advantage, from Kitty she never missed catching in her beak,
peanuts, kernels of corn or pennies. as they were tossed to
her.   She was a regular miser and pennies were hid in
crevices all over her room. she also stored up, the same as
wild jays do. quantities of food so as to be provided for a
rainy day

If I happened to be talking to anyone in the room, she would bide her time until we were not watching her, then swoop down between us so that a wing would sweep across our faces; if we were startled and dodged, as usually hap-

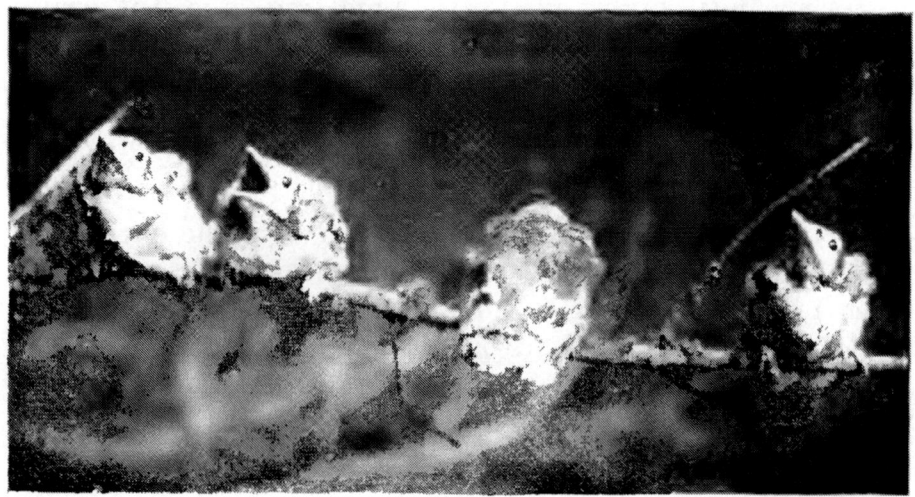

Fig. 78. *Three days before they left the nest, of their own accord*

pened, she would dance up and down and whistle in her ecstacy. She was fond of bright colored objects, especially if they were on ladies' hats. One day a lady went into the room wearing imitation cherries on her hat. Kitty was quite fond of cherries but had never had them served that way before. She did not, however, complain about the service but landed right in the middle of the bunch and commenced to hammer away with all her might. Fortunately for me, I got her away before any damage was done.

One day a live Barred Owl was brought to me and was placed in the room outside of Kitty's portion. Kitty's greatest delight was to escape from her apartment when we opened the door to feed her. By a sudden dash, she got her freedom on the day the owl was brought in. She had

never seen an owl before but was perfectly willing to take
a chance on hectoring him. Every time she flew across the
room she would whistle with glee as he opened his eyes and
blinked at her. The owl made no attempt to dissuade her
from her play but I imagine he was saying to himself: "You
just wait until night, you little blue imp, and I'll wring
your neck." Of course as Kitty was safely fastened in her
own apartment before dark, the owl had no opportunity to
get his revenge.

It is a pity that such beautiful and interesting birds as
Blue Jays should be so destructive. They do a great deal
of useful work in destroying caterpillars but the harm they
work in destroying eggs and young of other useful birds
much more than balances the good that they do. Still I
think that no one would advocate the extermination of jays;
certainly not until that greatest of all pests, the English
Sparrow is gotten rid of.

Fig. 79. NEST OF RUBY-THR. HUMMINGBIRD.

MOSS-COVERED HOMES

RUBY-THROATED HUMMINGBIRD.

Hummingbirds are creatures of the New World About five hundred species are found in North and South America. They range from Alaska to Patagonia, being most numerous in northern South America and in Central America. Only sixteen species out of this great number are known to have occurred in the United States and but a single species, the Ruby-throated Hummingbird, is found east of the Mississippi River.

I have always been greatly interested in these "gems." In fact, when I was but eight years of age my interest in them led me to capture one in a butterfly net as it flew about the flowers in the garden I thought I had a most wonderful prize but I am glad to say that my parents quickly induced me to release it As usual with all ornithologists at that time, my early investigations were made chiefly from a covetous standpoint. Much was learned, but knowledge so gained does not compare in value with that obtained when the possessive instinct is ignored

There is a very prevalent idea that Hummingbirds subsist entirely upon the honey or nectar of flowers; such a diet would soon ruin the digestive organs of any kind of bird or beast As a matter of fact, nectar forms a very small percentage of hummingbird food. Instead of sipping the honey from the flowers they visit, they usually are engaged in the very useful occupation of eating the many tiny insects that gather in such places. It is well known that most flowers that secrete nectar are partially or wholly dependent upon certain insects to carry pollen from one blossom to the stigma of another and so effect cross-fertilization; these useful insects are usually large, long-tongued ones like bees, moths and butterflies. So in destroying the tiny insects, hummingbirds perform a service to the plants by removing pilfering insects that do no good, and to mankind also.

Hummingbird

Fig. 80. FEMALE HUMMINGBIRD ON NEST.

I have always believed that nests of this hummingbird contain a greater amount of labor, are better made and are very much more beautiful than nests of any other kinds of birds I have had many excellent opportunities to watch them during their home-building

One day I saw a "hummer" buzzing about under some ferns, within a few inches of the ground; she was gathering the soft, downy wool that sheathes the young fronds and is often left hanging to the stems of older ferns. When she had a tiny load of this in her slender bill, she whizzed away with it; fortunately I was able to keep track of her rapid flight and saw her land on a limb about twenty feet above ground She had just commenced her work, barely enough of the future nest showing to be seen with the field glasses.

She was quite industrious but she only gathered tiny loads at a time and it took her quite a long while to find the material, so that building was a very slow operation At the end of three days, the walls of the nest had just commenced to assume a recognizable form.

Sometimes she brought little masses of whiter, finer material even than the "wool" probably cobwebs; this evidently held the balance of the material more closely together. I never saw her mate anywhere near the nest during its construction, but he did appear and help defend the home after the little "hummers" appeared.

The decorating of the outside of the nest was the most interesting part of the work. She seemed to be exceedingly particular about the appearance of each piece of lichen that was glued in place. Often she would buzz up and down and around the trunks of several trees before she could find a piece to her liking.

When finished, she had a bit of bird architecture of which she was justly proud Greens predominated in the lichens that grew on this tree, and all the pieces that were on her nest were of the same shade. Without seeing her going to it, nobody would have suspected that the little tuft of moss was other than a natural growth on the limb.

It was just ten days from the time the structure was commenced, when it was finished. In four days more, there were two little white eggs, just the size and shape of small pea-beans, laying in the soft little cup. In sixteen days

Fig. 81. *You can imagine how crowded this nest was before the first of the two young left.*

more, there emerged from these eggs, two tiny, naked mites, looked anything except like the little feathered jewels into which they were to develop. The little birds remained in the nest three weeks. At the end of the first week, tiny little pin feathers had commenced to appear; in two weeks they looked like little cushions stuck full of pins. From this time until they left, their feathers blossomed out very rapidly and they were transformed from the little helpless mites into lusty little birds bigger than the nest could comfortably hold

For two weeks they were fed entirely by regurgitation,—on food pre-digested by the parents. This feeding process is one of the most peculiar sights in bird-dom. The parent stands on the edge of the nest, erect and neck stretched to the utmost so as to get the slender bill into the mouth of the little one. The head is worked vigorously and the food "pumped in." It is a process that looks a great deal more like a surgical operation than like a dinner party.

Hummingbirds, tiny as they are, have violent and easily aroused tempers; no bird is more courageous nor as quick to attack man, bird or beast that threatens its home. With excited "chipperings," they will often dash right at your face like little winged bullets, so that you invariably dodge. They stop when a few inches away, but there is always the uncertainty so that one does not dare keep still to see if they would strike.

Hummers are quite cleanly in their habits. I never saw them bathe in pools of water, but I have seen them moistened as though with dew from the leaves, and then seen them taking "dust baths" to dry themselves. It is believed that our Hummingbird has a preference for bright red colors and that they like particularly well to feast from the depths of the cardinal flower, trumpet creeper and other gaudy, long-tubed blossoms of that hue. However, we find them very commonly about many of the garden and wild flowers of other colors and about apple, pear and cherry trees when they are in bloom.

Anna Hummingbird

One of the most common of the several hummingbirds found in California is called the Anna Hummingbird. It is slightly larger than our eastern bird and the male has a fiery-pink throat and crest,—a beautiful little species.

As a rule I believe that this species is even more tame

Fig. 82. ANNA'S HUMMINGBIRD.

than the Ruby-throat. I have known of many instances of
their flying to the flowers on ladies' hats. thinking that they
were real ones. They also show a partiality or preference
for a close acquaintance with mankind as they very often
build their nests in vines on trellises or piazzas of dwellings.
Their nests are made of woolly plant fibres held together,
especially on the outside with cobwebs. The outside has
little or no moss or lichen ornamentation. These nests are
usually built at low elevations, most often under ten feet
above ground, while I have found nests of the Ruby-
throat at least sixty feet up.

BLUE-GRAY GNATCATCHER.

These charming little birds are very common in the southern half of the United States. Their body is but little bigger than that of a hummingbird, but a rather long tail makes the total length of the bird a great deal more.

Their call notes can often be heard coming from the high trees that they like to frequent. It is a sound that would

Fig. 83. NEST OF BLUE-GRAY GNATCATCHERS.

escape the notice of many observers,—not loud and with an insect-like quality that might cause it to be overlooked,—a rather, twanging, high-pitched mew. Their song is a mixed medley of faint noises, not worthy of the name of a song, but it expresses their pleasure and, to them, it may be as beautiful as the efforts of our most accomplished musicians.

Although their vocal efforts may not appeal to us, they have two claims to notice that cannot be ignored,—their graceful beauty and their nest-building ability. Slim, graceful, with a soft blending of blue-gray, black and white, they create an impression that, coupled with their agility, matching that of the Chickadee, calls forth our admiration.

I have said that the nest of our hummingbird is one of the most beautiful bird creations. The Blue-gray Gnat-catcher nest is almost a perfect reproduction of the hummer-nest but on a much larger scale. While the nest of the hummingbird is small even in proportion to its maker, that of the gnatcatcher is rather large for the size of the bird; that is, the outside of the nest, the whole bulk of it. is large; but the walls are very thick so that the little, very deeply-cupped interior is hardly big enough to accomodate the little bird and the four or five beautiful, white, brown-specked eggs that she lays.

While you may see gnatcatchers feeding on the lower limbs of trees or among the underbrush. they like high elevations and it is usually high up in the trees, on horizontal branches, that the exquisite moss-covered homes are placed.

Wood Pewee.

Belonging to an entirely different family, but still building the same type of moss-adorned nest, is the Wood Pewee. These are among the commonest of the flycatchers; they are called pewees because of the song they sing so often during the summer months,—a very clearly whistled "pee-ah-wee; (short pause) peeeee-wee"

Nearly every small piece of woods has its pewees and often we find them in orchards. Each bird has a favorite perch or two,—dead twigs that give them a good view of the surrounding territory. They perch on these for hours at a time, occasionally dashing out after a luckless miller or bee that happens to pass within sight of their keen eyes;

Fig. 84.　NEST OF WOOD PEWEE.

ever and anon their plaintive "pee-ah-wee" rings out, often with clock-like regularity

It is, however, with Wood Pewee homes that we are at present concerned. These are, as I have said, moss-covered, but they are very inferior in construction to those either of the Hummingbird or Gnatcatcher. The bulk of the nest is made out of coarse plant fibres, not so perfectly quilted together and very shallow as compared to the nests of the other birds mentioned. The outside has less moss attached and it is not done in as firm a manner

Still these nests, saddling quite large limbs as they do, are very difficult to see. If one has patience they are, however, very easy to find, especially if the nest happens to contain a full set of the creamy white eggs with their sharp, brown specks. You have but to watch either of the owners. Should you chance to be observing the female, she will probably go to the nest within a few minutes; should it be the male bird that you are watching he will probably quite quickly betray the hiding place of the nest, for he is very attentive to his mate and often carries food to her as she sits on the eggs.

All flycatchers have a metallic little trill that they utter, usually when they are very happy and sometimes under stress of excitement; the female pewee gives it as she settles on her nest and the male usually does as he goes to feed her. I have found the greater number of their nests built on horizontal limbs of oak trees, but I have sometimes, too, found the· in chestnuts, in maples along roadsides and in apple trees. The majorit. have been located from twenty to fifty feet above ground, but I have found one as low as eight feet, this one being in an orchard.

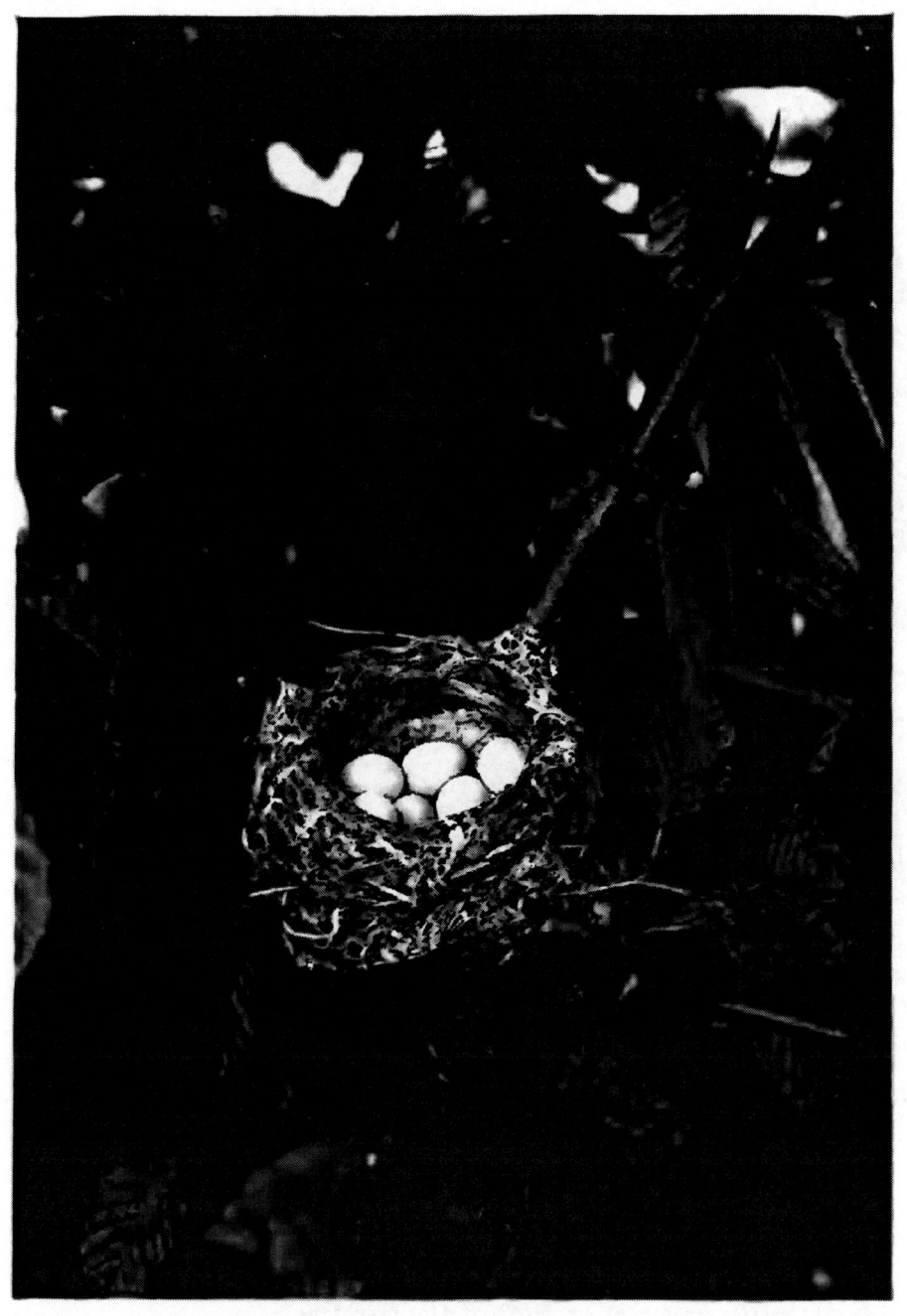

Fig. 85. NEST AND EGGS OF GOLDFINCH.

Fig 86. YOUNG GOLDFINCHES.

The adults in summer are often called Wild Canaries; their song is fully as sweet as that of the canary.

FAVORITE SONGSTERS

ROBIN

Were a vote to be taken to discover the most popular bird in America, fully three-quarters of them would probably be registered for the Robin. With the exception of Song Sparrows, no other birds found about cities and habitations, have as extensive a range. We may hear the same Robin song in Massachusetts, in California, in Alaska, in Labrador or in the Gulf States. To be sure, Robins are separated into three sub-species but it is only the hairsplitting ornithologist who can tell the difference between them and even he must know just where a Robin was taken before he can tell which kind it is.

Robins are migratory birds, but they migrate only just so far as is absolutely necessary in order to get food to live upon. Many of them pass the winter even in the north-

Fig. 87. ROBIN ON NEST.

Many nests are built in such locations.

Fig. 88.   ROBIN NEST.

A typical nest, the inside construction of which is almost wholly of mud.

ern states. where they can get shelter in large cedar swamps. It is quite probable that it is the birds from the extreme northern parts of their breeding range that winter in northern United States. while the birds that breed here migrate southwards to the Gulf States.

Fig. 89. JUST FED BUT STILL HUNGRY.

Adult Robins return to the same breeding grounds each year and are believed to remain mated for life. It is probable that the young birds become separated from their parents and from each other and seek new fields on their return from the south.

The song of the Robin is always pleasing,—a loud, rolling "cheer-up, cheerily cheerily. etc." varied greatly in pitch but usually fitting these words. An old rendition of the

Fig. 90. AN ATTRACTIVE LOCATION.

English Sparrows pulled the bottom from this nest and the eggs fell to the ground.

Robin song. probably originating in the mind of some phy-
sician, runs "Kill-him. cure-him; kill-him, cure-him; give
him physic; quick!" Robins have, however, other notes not
so pleasing. Their voices are loud and their lungs lusty.
When they have a real or fancied grievance they can create
more excitement and make more noise than a dozen of any
other species of bird. I can speak with authority in regard
to the volume of noise Robins are capable of making, for

Fig. 91. INSPECTION.

they consider placing a camera up in a tree within three
feet of their home, a real grievance and they call out all
other birds in the neighborhood to help them proclaim the
fact.

I well remember the first Robin nest I ever "tackled"
photographically, although it was a good many years ago.
It was on an apple bough perhaps ten feet above ground.
Tents were not used at that time. but the camera shutter

was operated from a distant hiding place. by means of a
very long tube and a very large bulb. This particular pair
of Robins never did like me. for I had. on several occasions,
visited nests in adjoining trees. so you can imagine the
greeting that I received when I climbed into their own tree,
pulled up the camera and set it with the great staring eye

Fig. 92. ARE THEY HUNGRY?

within three feet of their nest. I spent more time and
energy and had more trouble securing pictures of these particular Robins than I have ever experienced with any other
kind of birds. Curiously enough they did not care so much
about the camera which was so close to their home as they
did about me, hiding behind a tree a hundred feet away.
To make a long story short, I had to cover the camera with
my focussing cloth and leave it in that tree over night, returning the next morning with sufficient thread to operate

Fig. 93. *Taken in 1-100 of a second, showing the active movements of hungry young birds.*

the camera shutter from a distance of three hundred feet. I got the pictures but it was an unusual amount of trouble to do so, especially for such common birds as Robins. The different temperaments of different birds of the same species is emphasized by the fact that I have since taken Robin pictures with no concealment, from a distance of less than six feet.

Fig. 94. THE NEST ON THE BLIND.

Most normal Robins place their rudely constructed mud-and-grass houses in trees at heights of from six to twenty feet from the ground. Of course there are eccentric Robins, as well as persons, and some of these depart from the usual customs of their kind. We sometimes see their nests in the upper branches of elms, fully sixty feet up; I have also found them built among roots under overhanging banks.

Fig. 95. *Approaching the nest shown in figure 94.*

These represent the extremes of altitude. We have many instances of very odd locations a few of which I will mention.

Some people consider quantity rather than quality as the most important ingredient of music. Such must have been the opinions of the Robins that built their nest on a girder in a factory where the noise was continuous and deafening. They obtained entrance through a broken window pane opposite the girder. It is very strange that they should have had the temerity to even enter such a place and stranger still that they should choose it for their home.

A suburban trolley line crosses a brook over a short bridge

made by heavy iron stringers on which are wooden ties for the rails to rest upon. I think that if I were a bird and had determined to build a home in any such place, I should at least have placed it on one of the stringers between the ties where it would have had a secure foundation. Mrs. Robin, however, perhaps because she wanted more excite-

Fig. 96. *Sometimes worms were brought for the little ones and again mulberries from a nearby tree.*

ment and danger, plastered her nest right against the side of the rails, so that half rested on the lower flange and half on the tie. Cars ran on a half-hour schedule so that every fifteen minutes wheels rumbled over the rails within two inches of the rim of the nest. The strangest part of this nesting was that the nest remained in place and the young were successfully reared. While the Robin was incubating she always left the nest when cars passed over, at least during the daytime while I was watching; what she did at night can only be conjectured, but I presume from the actions of other birds under somewhat similar circumstances, that she stayed "aboard" the nest and let the cars go over her.

Another pair of Robins liked city life. They chose a spot in the very heart of a large city. where there were large lawns from which they could easily extract the earth worms so palatable to Robins, young and old, and also near a large mulberry tree; with these two handy sources of food

Fig. 97.   I WONDER IF THIS WILL SATISFY HIM.

supply they felt that they had an ideal location. The only objection was the numbers of English Sparrows that are always present in cities. The ruffians and our native song and insectivorous birds. through no fault of the latter, can seldom live peaceably in the same neighborhood. I think that these Robins may have previously met with the same misfortune that befell the pair that I will next tell about, and decided that the best way to avoid further trouble from that source was to trust to the protection of mankind. At

Fig. 98.   YOUNG ROBIN.

Showing the spotted breast common to the young of all members of the Thrush Family even though the adults have unmarked ones.

any rate, for three years in succession, they made their nest on the top of a blind on the front piazza of the property owner's house. As they were quite neat and did no damage they were allowed to remain and furnished a good deal of amusement for the family. The birds came and went without fear even while members of the family were gathered

Fig. 99. STILL HUNGRY.

on the piazza directly under the nest. Sparrows were not allowed about the house any more than possible, but sometimes bands of them would mob one of the Robins as it was bringing food to its young; the bird could protect itself, but usually lost its provender during the melee.

In the same city, another pair of Robins dwelt. They built their nest in an elm tree in front of a large block. A picture is shown of this Robin sitting upon the nest,—

Fig. 100. *Veery about to settle upon her greenish-blue eggs.*

taken from a window in the block. English Sparrows continually pestered this pair of birds. Although nesting material was abundant on every hand, the sparrows, out of pure deviltry, chose to steal it from the Robin rather than pick it up from the ground. One after another would slyly steal up under the nest. grasp the end of a straw or string, pull it from its fastening and, with a gleeful chuckle, fly away with it. These depredations continued until the bottom of the nest was torn out and the Robin eggs were dashed to the paving below.

Similar tragedies are enacted hundreds of times every year in all cities and towns yet we still sometimes meet misguided people who will undertake to defend the English Sparrow The person who can invent the surest, most effective and swiftest means of ridding our country of these pests will be one of the greatest benefactors of mankind.

Veery or Wilson Thrush

As in the case of a great many of our birds, it is from its song that this species receives its name. This song is a descending spiral of tremulous. reedy whistles, which may be interpreted as "Vee-r-r-r-r-y. vee-r-r-r-r-y," the 'veery' being repeated perhaps half a dozen times, each making a complete turn of the spiral and each being of a lower pitch and lesser volume than the preceding. This song may be heard at almost all hours of the day and often until after dusk in most woodland, during summer. Their call and note of protest is a single, tremulous, mournful, ascending whistle.

Veeries are perfectly garbed for the life they lead, on or near the ground, their backs being almost a perfect match in color to dead leaves

Veeries build their nests of strips of bark and fine grasses, placing them on the ground or very near it; often it is set down in the middle of a patch of dead leaves, sometimes in the midst of a clump of ferns and often against the sides or in the middle of old stumps. The four greenish-blue eggs loom up prominently in the deeply-cup-ped nest; probably for that reason the bird does not leave the nest unless she is seen, for to do so would expose the brightly colored eggs to view and result in discovery while she can usually escape notice.

Although I have taken many pictures of Wilson Thrushes in many different locations, the one chosen for this sketch

Fig. 101. VEERY RETURNING TO NEST.

illustrates one of my very first attempts at bird photogra-phy. This nest was situated at the base of a clump of black-berry vines, and contained four eggs. The bird proved to be more shy than usual and in two weeks time I was able to secure but two satisfactory pictures of her.

The day following its discovery an attempt was made to picture the Thrush returning to the nest. The camera was set with the lens but two feet distant from the eggs and I was concealed in a heap of brush twenty feet away. The camera was covered with a green cloth and plentifully sprinkled with leaves so as to attract as little attention as possible, but undoubtedly it looked to the Veeries bigger than a house would to us.

Both birds were away while I was getting in readiness. Upon their return they were greatly astonished to see a strange affair standing so near their home. They talked to each other about it, in low tones, for several minutes and then flew away. In about ten minutes they returned, talk-

Fig. 102. VEERY ON NEST.

ed some more and went off again. Evidently they thought the camera was something that would remove its unwelcome presence after awhile and they were going to wait for it to go.

Just twice during the three days that I was present while the nest contained eggs, did the owner visit it, that is to actually alight upon the nest. Upon developing the first exposure, the nest and eggs appeared beautifully but there was not a trace of the Veery although she was standing on the edge of the nest when I pressed the bulb. The second

Fig. 103. VEERY FEEDING HER YOUNG.

exposure was the one shown here. of the Veery entering the nest.

The next morning the eggs had hatched. I waited until the little birds were ten days old before attempting to again photograph the parent. She was still very shy but remained in sight of the nest all the time. usually with her beak filled with food for her babies. Her mate perched on a branch hard by and, after scolding for awhile. tried to induce her to be brave by singing to her. Sometimes his "veery" song would ring out exceedingly loud and clear, and again it would be just a faint murmur as though the singer were a great ways off, although he sat on the same twig about thirty feet distant.

Finally Mrs. Veery descended to the ground and commenced walking in a circle about the nest, each circuit bringing her a little nearer the goal. Every time she came to the slender tube running from the camera to my place of concealment she would pause and look at it critically. then jump over it and turn quickly about to look it over again. With her head cocked to one side so comically, I could imagine her saying to herself: "It looks like a worm, but it can't be, for I never heard of one as long as that is." At last she hopped to the nest, all the little heads were expectantly raised, mouths wide open like little yellow caverns, and my long awaited opportunity had come.

Several times we went through this operation but with the exception of the picture shown here. the results were not satisfactory to me. Several incidents happened to relieve the monotony of waiting,—incidents that tended to still further alarm and delay the return of an already shy mother bird. The thrush was just on the point of approaching the nest when a fusilade of shots was heard from the edge of the woods. Soon a twenty-five year old, overgrown boy appeared armed with a small repeating rifle. He passed by about twenty yards distant and showed his sporting

Fig. 104. *You can sometimes approach and take a "time" picture of a Wood Thrush without alarming her.*

prochvities by firing at every animate object, when his supply of these ran short he would even shoot at the surrounding trees, just for excitement I kept close watch to see that he did not notice the camera for he certainly would have tried to hit it, although his enthusiasm far exceeded his skill for he missed everything that he fired at while in my sight.

The next diversion was occasioned by one of the several cows that were feeding in the swamp She ambled over to the camera and persisted in eating the leaves off the branches with which I had covered it, and seemed to take it unkindly when I was forced to drive her away to protect the camera.

Wood Thrush

This is the largest and handsomest of our true thrushes and, in my estimation, has a much sweeter and more pleasing song than any of the others, not excepting the famous Hermit Thrush that I have often heard both in breeding grounds and during migrations. The Wood Thrush song is one impossible of adequate description,—clear and flutelike, the notes coming after regular pauses, usually in groups of threes, the last one of which is often held and vibrated These birds are heard at their best early in the morning and again just as darkness closes in about the woods

The Wood Thrush nest reminds one somewhat of that of the Robin A small percentage of mud also enters into its construction but not nearly as much as Robins use The bulk of the nest is composed of grasses, rootlets and a few leaves It is usually located in underbrush, where it is shaded by taller trees, at heights of from six to ten feet from the ground The birds are usually very tame while setting, often allowing you to touch them before they will leave the nest After they have left, however, it is difficult to induce them to return while you are near I have not

124

Fig. 105. YOUNG WOOD THRUSH.

yet been able to photograph them feeding their young, probably because I have not yet met the "right" bird.

While eggs of the Veery are of a greenish-blue, resembling in size and shape those of Catbirds, eggs of the Wood Thrush are of that peculiar color known as "Robin-egg' blue and most nearly resemble eggs of Robins.

Fig. 106. WOOD THRUSH ON NEST.

They sit so closely that sometimes you may touch them before they will leave the eggs.

ROSE-BREASTED GROSBEAK.

The male of this species is always popular with bird lovers, for he is very handsome, is always cheerful and has a beautiful song. The female is popular too with those who know her, but she is dressed so differently from her mate and so inconspicuously, like a big sparrow, that she is seldom noticed. The Grosbeak song is similar to, but readily

Fig. 107.   NEST OF GROSBEAK

The eggs are pale greenish-blue
blotched with reddish brown.

distinguished from and of better character than that of the
Robin.   His song is always preceded by a sharp chip, usually about two seconds before the song proper commences.

The Grosbeak nest is rather rudely and scantily constructed of rootlets.   It is normally placed in bushes or small
trees from six to fifteen feet up.   They, however, frequent-

Fig. 108.   FEMALE GROSBEAK ON NEST.

She looks like a big sparrow,—not at all like her beautiful mate.

ly make their homes within city limits and in such cases often build high up in large trees. The four eggs are greenish-blue, covered with brown spots.

The male grosbeak is considered, especially by the ladies, as a model bird-husband. He does at least half the work in constructing the home and he sits upon the eggs about as often and as long as his mate does. He is of a jovial disposition and likes his task so well that he commonly sings while sitting on the nest. I have located a number of their nests by searching for the singer. His song, when thus engaged is usually much lower in tone, as though he feared

128

Fig. 109. *Male Grosbeak with food for his tiny little ones.*

he would disclose the hiding place of the home, but he
must sing anyway.

I have often seen it stated that the female grosbeak sings,
too, but I have never seen one do so. The year-old males
very closely resemble the female in plumage. Probably it
is the songs of these young males that are often accredited
to the females. I was delighted on one day in June when
I happened to come across a Grosbeak nest at an elevation
of only about four feet from the ground. Here was the
opportunity I had been awaiting and I could, in imagination,
see a whole series of beautiful pictures illustrating the home
life of grosbeaks. Alas! The best of plans go astray. I

happened to have my camera with me when the nest was discovered and. as the female was at the time sitting on her eggs. I carefully moved up to within about four feet, focussed the camera and made an exposure of her. The next day I took my tent and complete outfit in order to get a good series of her approaching the nest. Not a sign of nest or eggs was in sight. Undoubtedly my "find" was found by some youthful oologist and the grosbeak nest and eggs went to grace (or disgrace) his cabinet.

Fig. 110. NEST OF CATBIRD.

Fig. 111. CATBIRD ON HER NEST.

BIRD MIMICS

CATBIRD

You cannot judge the disposition of a person by his clothes, neither can you judge that of a bird by its feathers. A soft gray suit and black cap is the garb worn by the Catbird,—raiment that might indicate its wearer to be a quiet, Quaker-like bird although in reality no other has a more irascible temper than our Catbird. A perfect model of propriety when everything is in accord with his temperament but a real virago and scold when the least thing goes amiss.

I always like to listen to the Catbird song. It is a song

Fig. 112. *A real virago if you provoke her to anger; and her ire is very easily aroused.*

132

Fig. 113. *Her eyes snap as they watch your every move. Not a sound from her until she leaves the nest,—then beware.*

such as no other bird is capable of giving. The Mockingbird has a clearer, sweeter and more lengthy song but it cannot compare with that of the Catbird in its variety of notes, musical and otherwise, or the absolute indifference to rhyme, rhythm or reason with which it is delivered. The song cannot be written or even adequately described for it is never twice alike and seems to be made up on the spur of the moment.

They often perch in the tops of bushes and sing for an
hour or more at a time,—wings and tail drooping, head
erect and eyes half closed. From between the half-opened
bills, come selections from the songs of robins, thrushes,
of wagon wheels, mewing of cats, clucking and cackling
of hens and noises of his own invention like nothing ever
before heard.

Fig. 114. NO SIGN OF FEAR IN THIS POSE.

Catbirds build quite large and substantial nests of small
twigs, rootlets and shreds of bark; the bowl-shaped interior is lined with slender black rootlets and on these the four
greenish-blue eggs are laid. The female is very loathe to
leave her nest while setting and will usually allow anyone
to almost touch her before she glides off the eggs. Once

off, however, her anger is unrestrained and she gives her
opinion of you in strident tones that alarm the bird population for a long distance around. Catbird anger is not ex-
pressed solely in noise either; I have seen a chipmunk running for his life to escape from the attacks of a pair that
had caught him in the bushes near their nest; I have seen
them dash furiously at a black snake, that was hunting
among the branches for egg-dainties, until he was forced to

Fig. 115. YOUNG CATBIRD.

slip to the ground and flee; and I have had one of them come
screaming at me and peck at my fingers as I reached
through the briers to feel what was in a nest. Their most
effective note of protest is a loud, whining "tschay" repeated as fast as they can get their breath and sometimes
drawn out into a continuous scream.

My experiences at photographing Catbirds have been
many and varied; I have had a lot of the experience and
got but few of the pictures. I have not yet induced one to
return and feed its young while I had a camera in position

Fig. 116.   BROWN THRASHER ON NEST.

before the nest. When without a camera I have, a number
of times, hidden beside Catbird nests and watched the
parents performing their various household duties. There
are "good" Catbirds and "bad" ones; it is just as impossible
to photograph one of the latter class as it is to portray a
naughty child.

BROWN THRASHER

The Thrasher is also something of a mimic but not as accomplished a performer in that line as the Catbird. He
has, however, a much better and more characteristic song of
his own.

Early one morning I was making my way along a side
hill, through sweetfern and briers and around scrub oaks

136

Fig. 117.   NEST AND EGGS OF BROWN THRASHER.

and thorn bushes. The shadow of a bird overhead caused
me to glance up just in time to see the long, bright-rufous
tail of a Thrasher disappear in a bush a short distance away.
Naturally as I passed, I parted the leaves to see what she
was doing there. I was scarcely prepared for the "hornet-
nest" that I had disturbed. An angry Thrasher confronted
me, her bright yellow eyes blazing with wrath, her wings

Fig. 118.   ON GUARD.

and tail wide spread. From her cavernous mouth came a
continuous stream of explosive "chirks," angry, grating
"Karr-r-r-r's" and clearly whistled "wheu's." I had in-
terrupted her as she was giving her children their break-
fasts and a Catbird or Thrasher meal cannot be disturbed
with impunity.

I stood perfectly still and she scolded until she became
tired; she gradually quieted down, her ruffled feathers as-

Fig. 119. *She sometimes fed them great black ants.*

sumed their normal positions and the angry glint left her
eyes. She began to wonder what she had been making all
the fuss about anyway. I whistled softly to her and, after
looking at me steadily for a few moments, she answered in
the same tone. In a few moments more she cleaned the
nest and left with no concern for my presence.

I had been on the way to photograph some towhees
about half a mile farther on but I decided to let the latter
go a day or two and set up my green tent beside the
Thrasher nest. I had it in readiness before she returned

and she paid not the slightest regard to it but went directly
to the nest. Unfortunately the sun shining through the
leaves caused a spotty background and made many shadows
about the nest. Usually it is possible to tie branches out
of the way so as to get good surroundings and light, but in
this case they would not admit of so doing

Fig. 120. *Spiders, too, were often brought to appease the
hunger of the little thrashers.*

The three young birds were about a week old,—just large
enough to commence to take an interest in things going
on about them. They had very acute and discriminating
hearing, other birds were singing in all directions about us
but they always heard mother Thrasher's low whistle,

usually given when she was twenty or thirty feet away from the nest. They would prick up their ears and with wide-open eyes and mouths opened wider still, each strive to be the nearest to her as she hopped to the back edge of the nest.

Mother Thrasher showed no intentional partiality but fed her three children in turn. Occasionally she made a

Fig. 121. *Sometimes Thrashers nest on the ground but more often in bushes.*

mistake and fed the same one twice in succession. As the little fellows grew older they resented such slights. The one whose turn it was to be fed would raise his voice in noisy protest if a nice, appetizing spider was, by mistake, thrust down his brother's throat. As the morsel was immediately swallowed he had no redress except to peck at his brother as soon as his mother left.

Father Thrasher must have been on a vacation the day that I found this nest for I did not see him, but he was in evidence on several subsequent days. I never saw him feed the little ones, though as a rule both parents share the task between them. His plumage was in perfect condition, while that of the female Thrasher was worn and several

Fig. 122. YOUNG BROWN THRASHERS.

tail feathers were missing, showing that she had borne the brunt of the hard work and perhaps fought most of the battles of life too.

It was during the last week in May that I found the foregoing nest. The little birds had left it and were scratching for themselves early in June, while their parents undertook to raise another family. This time they selected a place only a short distance from the first one, but they built the nest on the ground instead of in the thorn bush that stood over it. From the appearance of her plumage, I am sure that the female Thrasher was the same one that I had been photographing. Either her memory was very poor or someone had frightened her, for she failed to be friendly with me any more and refused to return to the second nest while I was near.

Fig. 133. CEDAR WAXWING ON NEST.

BIRDS OF SILENCE

Cedar Waxwing

Cedar Birds or "Cherry Birds" as they are very often called, unfortunately are connoisseurs of fine fruit, particularly of the various kinds of cultivated and wild cherries. Unfortunately, too, owners of such trees seldom take any interest in birds except to regard as undesirable all that sometimes steal their fruit. There is no question but what the birds do considerable damage to the cherry crop, consequently it is difficult to reason the farmer out of his habit of setting his hired boy to guarding the trees with a shot gun. Cherries last but a short time and, during the remainder of the year, Cedarbirds eat quantities of insects especially canker worms that are so destructive to orchards.

Except during the nesting season they go about in flocks of from six to twenty individuals. The most marked peculiarity about them is their silence. A flock of fifteen or twenty may perch in a wild cherry tree by the hour and not a sound will indicate their presence unless it be the occasional dropping of a cherry. Their only call is a nasal hissing or whistling audible for but a short distance.

They remain in flocks until the nesting season, which commences the latter part of June. Even then they often congregate in their favorite cherry trees, but they come and go as individuals.

Their nests are constructed of weeds, grasses, rootlets and moss, skilfully woven together and lined with fine grasses. Although nearly as large as robin nests they are not nearly as easily seen for they are usually cunningly concealed in clusters of leaves. Orchard trees furnish their most frequently chosen nesting sites.

On the fifteenth day of one June, a Cedar Waxwing was observed gathered web from a caterpillar nest. This was carried to an old, lone apple tree standing near the wall in a large field. No investigation was made at the time, but

Fig. 124. NEST OF WAXWING.

They are very often placed in orchard trees.   The composition is chiefly of grasses and string with considerable moss worked into it.   The eggs are a gray-blue with black specks.

the occurrence was noted to be looked up later. On June thirtieth search of the tree revealed a typical Cherry-bird nest containing four dull bluish eggs with few black spots.

This pair of Cedar-birds made an unfortunate choice of a nesting site, for they had built their house on two crossing limbs. Every time the wind blew, their house tipped back and forth and threatened to spill the contents out. As we did not wish such a calamity to happen, we tied the branches together and then, as an additional precaution, tied the nest more firmly in place. Probably the birds did not appreciate this kindness but it undoubtedly saved the lives of their little ones as will be seen later. While we were engaged in making over their home as we thought it should be, the two Cedar-birds perched on the topmost branches and feebly protested.

It was twenty days before we again visited the nest. We could see from a distance that it was safe and that the parent birds were busy feeding little ones. They both left and flew about overhead until they calmed sufficiently to alight on their lookout perches and watch to see what we were about.

As soon as the branch was touched, up flew four heads with wide open mouths the interior of which was blood-red in color,—very different from that of the young of other birds. They were repulsive little things,—closed eyes, skin like soft black leather and not a sign of feathers about them.. As soon as they found that no food was forthcoming, they cuddled down in the bottom of the nest and remained quiet while we were making our preparations.

The limbs were weighted with a large stone so as to bring the nest down to a height of about five feet, all intervening branches were tied out of the way and the one that shaded the nest had a string attached so that it could be pulled to one side and let sunlight strike the nest when we wished.

After seeing that the picture was satisfactory on the

Fig. 125.   *Sometimes cherries were fed in their whole state, and again they were crushed.*

ground glass we retired to the other side of the wall. We found that we needed no concealment; as long as we were out of sight from the tree, the Cedar-birds considered it safe to go to and from the nest without regard to us. After the female had looked the nest over carefully and found that we had not harmed the little ones she flew away leaving her mate on guard.

Upon her return, the two parents talked matters over a few minutes and then she slyly hopped down, branch by branch, until she was beside the nest. Although to all appearances she had brought no food, she had a plentiful supply concealed in her throat Cedar-birds feed their young by regurgitation; sometimes the food is administered to the little ones in a well masticated state and again it may be in the raw condition.

As she stepped to the edge of the nest all the young heads were elevated and she assumed an attitude of inspection, watching them intently for a few moments possibly to see which was the most in need of food As each was reaching its very highest and opening its mouth to the greatest possible extent it seemed to be a difficult proposition to decide. At last she made a convulsive movement of the head and,—a bright red cherry appeared in her bill. This was quickly thrust down the throat of the nearest little bird; as it was not instantly swallowed she took it away from him and gave it to the next one If there is not immediate muscular response in the throat of a young bird, food is at once withdrawn and given to one in a fit condition to receive it; this is done at least by all the song and insectivorous birds with which I am familiar.

Cedar-birds seem to do everything systematically. One of these always remained on guard and the other joined two more that flew overhead at regular intervals, the three going to a cherry tree about a quarter of a mile away where they managed to find some belated fruit. The politeness of

Fig. 126. *She would look at them intently as though to decide which was the most in need of food.*

Cedar-birds has frequently been noted. Often when a number are feeding, one will seize a cherry, pass it to the next and this one in turn give it to his neighbor. A number of times I have seen cherries thus go the rounds of three or four birds before they were swallowed.

On the return trip, our bird would leave and drop down to the topmost twig of the apple tree while the other two continued down into the valley where they had their homes. Mother Wax-wing fed the little birds several times while her mate kept watch. She was not a bird to be imposed on for very long, however; after calling to him for some time she flew to his side and pecked at him until he went down to the nest and gave his children the cherries he had been holding in his mouth for so long. She went along with him and we secured a good view of the group just as he was "coughing up" some food.

During this day the parent birds fed the young at intervals of about ten minutes for half an hour, then the mother brooded them for the next half hour. Two days later we had a violent thunder storm accompanied by very high winds. I very much feared for the safety of the nest and its occupants and was very glad to find later that our strings had held things in place, although the nest was a little awry.

As we approached the parents left the nest and the young birds, now almost large enough to fly, assumed the same motionless attitude, heads well forward, that the adults always take when startled.

I never before had young birds act as these did when we placed them side by side on a branch. They were all as "mean" as they could be but one of them was a regular imp; just like a spoiled child, he would bite and kick and throw himself backwards off the branch, regardless of how he fell,—usually, however, he would grab a neighbor by the wing or tail and pull it along with him. When we could get them to stay on the branch at all, they looked stiff and

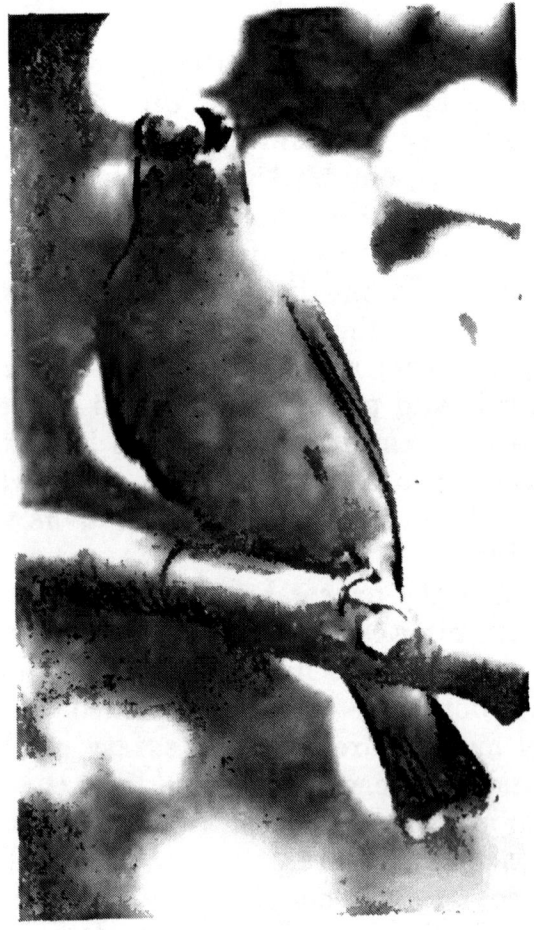

Fig. 127. RIPE CHERRIES.

unnatural, just like stuffed images. The three little Cedar-birds in the picture that is shown belong to another family; they behaved beautifully, sat perfectly still and would each turn its head just where we wanted it. Unfortunately the parents of these birds could not be induced to return and feed them, while the ones that owned the unruly children would alight on the branch and feed the single little bird we could induce to remain still.

Fig. 128 *The little birds were mean subjects; they simply would not pose.*

The birds usually brought two three or four cherries at a time in their throats. They did not. however. feed the little Cedar-birds entirely upon cherries for they sometimes brought different species of moths and caterpillars. Often while one was perched on the lookout twig awaiting the return of its mate, it would dash into the air and snap up a passing insect; sometimes these would be taken to the young, but more often would be eaten by the captor.

Fig. 129.   YOUNG CEDARBIRDS.

CUCKOOS.

Two species of Cuckoos are commonly found in eastern North America, the Black-billed and the Yellow-billed. The former is the most abundant in the northern half of the United States and the latter in the southern half. The two species are very easily distinguished although beginners in bird study often get them confused. The Yellow-billed Cuckoo is the largest, has a yellow lower mandible and the outer tail-feathers are black with broad white tips. The Black-billed species has an entirely black bill and the tail is a uniform olive-brown with narrow white tips to the outer feathers.

Both species build very shabby nests,—mere platforms of a few twigs, usually lined with a few catkins. The eggs of the Yellow-billed species are considerable larger and paler colored than those of the other. Three or four eggs is a normal set. These are deposited at very irregular intervals, sometimes several days intervening between layings. The bird often commences to set when only one egg is laid,

153

Fig. 130.   NEST OF BLACK-BILLED CUCKOO.

therefore it is very common to find eggs and young birds in the nest at once or young varying greatly in size.

Our cuckoos do not lay their eggs in nests of other birds, but always build their own nests. European Cuckoos, which belong to a different genus, do not build nests but lay their eggs in nests of other birds. Much confusion exists

Fig. 131. BLACK-BILL'S NEST AMONG BRIERS.

on this subject because writers getting their ideas from English books speak of the Cuckoo as a parasite and even school teachers often ignorantly inform their pupils of this fact which is not true concerning our birds. The only bird-parasite we have is the Cowbird.

I have included Cuckoos under "Birds of Silence" because they are very slow and quiet in their actions and do not often use their voices. but they can sing. or rather they have notes which can hardly be called songs. The tones of the two species are very similar but one familiar with them can always tell which kind it is by the sound and the rhythm. The Black-bill has regular intervals between the

Fig. 132. NEST OF YELLOW-BILLED CUCKOO.

"kow-kow's" while the Yellow-bill usually rapidly retards his.

Although Cuckoos build homes and care for their young after a fashion. they do not have the attachment for them that most birds do for their little ones. I have not yet, out of probably half a dozen trials. succeeded in getting one to return either to the eggs or to feed young when I was pre-pared for picture-making. Some day I expect to find one whose home ties are stronger. They do, however, have a degree of affection for one another as the following will show:

Fig. 133. YELLOW-BILL'S—JUST HATCHING.

Cuckoos are very fond of tent caterpillars, in fact they eat more of these hairy creatures than all the rest of the birds together. One day I saw a Black-bill Cuckoo sitting beside a large caterpillar nest. He would utter a few notes and then eat a few caterpillars. Evidently he intended to stay by his find until they were all gone. After a while he took one in his bill and flew into a thicket a short distance away. In a few moments he was back again and after regaling himself for awhile, off he went with another mouth-

Fig. 134. FIRST STAGE—PIN FEATHERS.

Fig. 135. SECOND STAGE—Quills.

ful. I carefully walked around the thicket and quietly
parted the leaves. He was just returning with another
caterpillar protruding from either side of his bill. He did
not notice me and came directly to his nest which proved to
be only about six feet from me. Instead of giving the morsel to young Cuckoos as I had expected, he passed it to his

Fig. 136. AT LAST—FEATHERS.

mate who, as I afterwards learned, was closely sitting upon
her four blue eggs. It was an act of devotion that, knowing Cuckoos as I thought I did, I had not expected to see. I
have always thought that had not somebody or something
taken the eggs from this nest, it would have furnished me
with the opportunity to have gotten some successful pictures.

ONLY SPARROWS.

"Oh, I only saw a Robin a Bluebird and a lot of sparrows!" I have heard similar expressions many a time It is amazing to find what a very large percentage of the people regard any brown bird as 'just a sparrow' There are a lot of sparrows, but they are all quite different in plumage and some of them are very beautiful Nearly all of them have beautiful plumage or interesting songs There should be just as much interest taken in the study of the sparrows as in the warblers or any other family of birds The reason for this sort of apathy concerning them is probably due to the very abundance and undesirable qualities of the English Sparrows that infest our streets everywhere

CHIPPING SPARROW.

On June twenty-seventh, a Chipping Sparrow was seen flying through a small growth of pines. This was nothing unusual for Chipping Sparrows were plentiful about the place, but this bird had a green worm in its beak; consequently she was kept under observation until she disappeared in the top of a little pine. The voices of little birds could be heard in the same spot, but so well was the nest concealed that several circuits of the tree failed to reveal it.

Carefully parting the boughs at the top. we opened to view the pretty scene of the mother Chippy, standing on the edge of a nest. admiring her family of four She seemed to show neither anger nor fear at the interruption but viewed us with as much interest as we did her It was a strange fact that this pair of birds. nesting more than half a mile from the nearest habitation, showed less fear than a pair that dwelt in a public park where people were constantly passing within three feet of them.

It was a very bright looking lot of little ones. reared in this cozy and secure home, where the sunlight filtered down

Fig. 137. A CHIPPY PORTRAIT.

Perfectly fearless, he stood between his little ones and the camera although the latter was but three feet away.

Fig. 138. NEST OF CHIPPING SPARROW.

They build most frequently in orchard trees; the eggs are pale blue with black specks.

through the same needles that protected them from the breezes that always swept across the top of the hill. The nest was made of small black rootlets and lined with the horsehair that is ever-present in nests of Chipping Sparrows. Besides the four young there was, in the nest, one egg, pale blue with small black specks on the large end, which had not hatched.

The male Chippy returned to the nest within five minutes after the camera had been focussed. We used no tent nor concealment of any kind,—simply stood behind the camera

11

and worked the shutter with the ordinary bulb and tube. They were the very tamest birds with which I have ever dealt, which accounts in part for the excellent results that were obtained photographically at this nest.

At his first visit the male bird brought no food, but just

Fig. 139. *Both adult birds came and went freely, without regard to our presence.*

came to see that the little ones were all right. The picture entitled "A Chippy Portrait" represents the result of the first 'shot', showing him as he was inspecting the camera.

He did not move while plates were being changed, but just as we were in readiness for another exposure, his mate was seen coming with a green worm, and he left. As she

Fig. 140. *They reached eagerly for the green worm Mother Chippy brought.*

reached the edge of the nest all the young birds rushed to meet her. They were so very eager, each to receive the morsel she brought that they very nearly spoiled the next picture by their rapid motions. We made but five pictures at this time and two of these were worthless because both the adults and little ones moved too fast for the shutter.

The following day was one of those rare, perfect days for photographs,—very light, but the sky sufficiently over-

Chipping Sparrow

Fig. 141. PREPARING BREAKFAST. *A very unusual sight and*
The parent birds breaking in two a caterpillar that was too large.
perhaps never before photographed

cast to prevent any shadows. At nine o'clock we were back in the grove to see our new acquaintances. Although the young had appeared very 'smart' the day before, we were, nevertheless, surprised to find that they had all left the nest. Two of them were sitting, side by side, on a small dead limb of a neighboring tree, but the other two were not in sight.

Fig. 142. *Food is pushed down the throats of the young—not simply dropped into their mouths.*

After watching the old birds for quite a while, we at last located the missing pair and returned them to the side of their mates, who had already been carefully focussed in the camera. After having once tested their wings and found that they could fly for short distances, they were not content to sit still, especially just where we wanted them to. Time after time, they made short excursions and had to be brought back.

The adults did not seem to be greatly alarmed as to the safety of the little ones we were handling so much and, after we had them arranged to our satisfaction and had stepped back, one of them flew away after food. He was back very quickly and at once went to feed the little birds, while his mate started off to hunt too. They continued this routine for a long time, one going as soon as the other came in sight.

Fig. 143. *This is one of the failures, but it shows the amount of movement that occurred in 1-100 of a second,—wings from side to their highest point.*

Our illustrations show a picture of father Chippy as ne pushed a whole beak-full of plant lice down the throat or one of his offspring and also of the mother as she delivered her antidote for hunger. You will notice that in both these pictures there is a 'vacant chair'; one of the little fellows could not overcome his desire to aviate and had to be chased about every five minutes.

They came and went in turn, so regularly that we concluded that if we could detain one of the adults for a few minutes we would have them both arriving at the same time. The scheme worked to perfection. We prevented the fe· male from feeding the young until the male was seen com-

Fig. 144. A LONG REACH.

Notice that the adult is reaching over two little birds and the space where another one should be.

ing in the distance, and as a result, secured the picture entitled "The Chippy Family". Mother, on the right of the picture, has just fed the two birdies nearest to her and is turning to leave just as father arrives with a beautiful green worm for the remaining little ones. I regard this as the best bird photograph that I ever secured; every one of the six birds is absolutely sharp, even to the finest feathers. Only those who have made bird pictures can realize how slight a movement will show on the plate.

The next appearance of the two birds at the same time is shown in "Preparing Breakfast". This shows one of the occurrences in bird-life that is very rarely witnessed and still less often photographed. The male bird is the one nearest the young; he had just fed the little one beside him and was on the point of leaving when the female arrived with a large caterpillar. To our surprise, instead of alighting on the other side of the little birds, as usual, she

Fig. 145.   AN ANTIDOTE FOR HUNGER.

lit at the side of her mate. In bird language, she instructed him what to do, and the next moment he had hold of one end of the caterpillar, bearing down with all his might; she lifted up on her end until it parted in the center. The two youngsters in the middle , who have anticipation written on every line of their faces, were the recipients of the broken morsel.

   We were also fortunate in being able to reproduce another very interesting performance, shown in the picture entitled "A Long Reach". You will notice that the little bird with

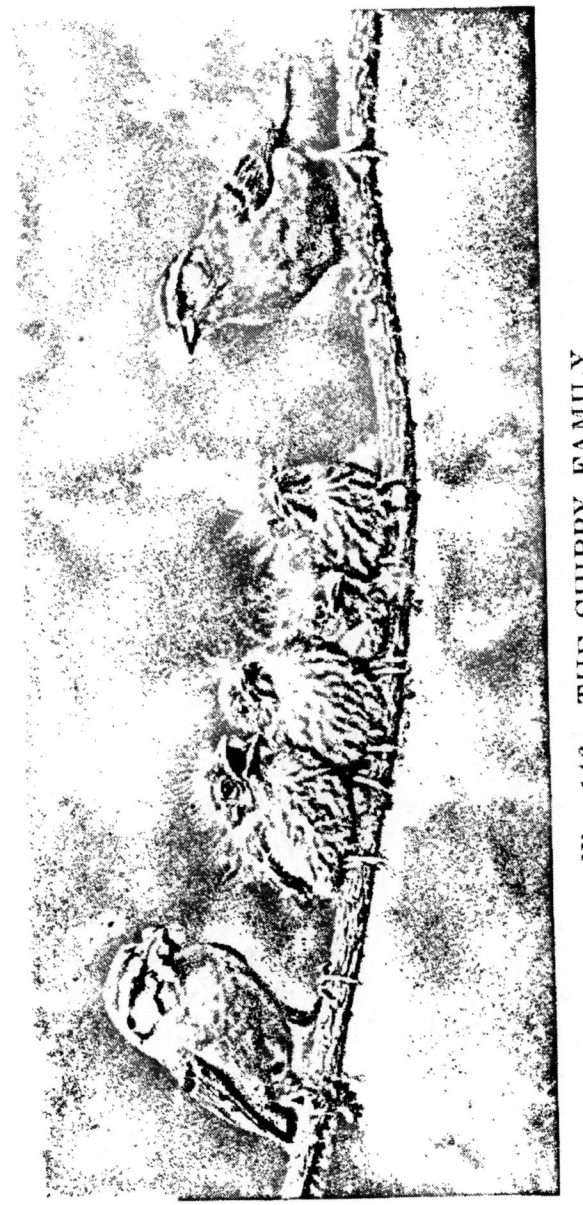

Fig. 146.   THE CHIPPY FAMILY.

It is very unusual to secure a photograph of an entire family of birds and have all of them perfectly sharp in every detail.

which we have had so much trouble, has taken another flight and is missing. The mother is just turning to go, and shows a slight motion in the picture. The father is reaching entirely over two birds and the space where the other should have been, to feed the one farthest away from him. It is no mean acrobat, who can thus maintain his equilibrium with his center of gravity falling so far outside his support.

One never knows until after the plates are developed, whether he has secured success or failure, when engaged in bird photography, so we exposed about two dozen plates, of which more than half came out satisfactorily, the poor ones being due to too rapid motion on the part of the subjects

These birds may be "only sparrows" but they are very interesting ones, as anyone seeing them as we did, would have to admit.

Song Sparrow.

Go where you will, throughout the length and breadth of our land and still you will find Song Sparrows. In the deserts of southwestern United States is a very pale colored race that matches perfectly the soil and surroundings. In northwestern United States and British Columbia is a very dark Song Sparrow,—in fact all the birds from that region are darker than the same species are from other sections of the country. In Alaska is a very large Song Sparrow,—a veritable giant when compared to our eastern one.

Everywhere you will find that the habits of these birds are practically alike and their songs are nearly enough like those of our common eastern bird to be easily recognized.

The song of the Song Sparrow has been set to a good many words; the one that always most appealed to me is the "Molly, put the teakettle-ettle-ettle on and we'll all take tea-ee-ee"; words that do not mean much on paper, but easily fit in place when you are listening to the song as rendered by the bird.

These birds are not at all particular in regard to their nesting sites. Usually they conceal their homes in thick clumps of grass or weeds, or in bushes not far from the ground, but I have found them in fields where there was not a spear of grass to offer shade and on ledges that were almost bare.

Although Song Sparrows are among our most common birds and their nests are very easy to find, I have made but very few pictures of them, chiefly because I have always had other nests to occupy what time I had at my disposal. On

Fig. 147. NEST OF SONG SPARROW.

Fig. 148. SONG SPARROW.

a number of occasions when I have been without a camera
I have found individual birds that were exceedingly tame,
in fact I have had several alight on my hand to feed little
birds that I was holding. Others have allowed me to stroke
them on the back as they were sitting on their nests, but
of course such instances are unusual, for Song Sparrows
usually chirp and scold vigorously if anyone comes near
their home.

FIELD SPARROW.

As would be judged from their name, these birds are in-
habitants of fields,—not fields carpeted with fresh green
grass, though, but dry side hills or hollows that are usually
plentifully sprinkled with small shrubs.

Throughout the East, the high-pitched, piping melody
that constitutes their song is one of the most familiar
sounds of rural districts. Commencing with a single long-
drawn whistle of intermediate pitch, it continues through
a succession of three or four very high notes and ends in a
pleasing little trill. It is a rather pretty little song

Fig. 149. FIELD SPARROW.

that once heard will not likely be forgotten or confused with
that of any other bird.

They nest about equally often on the ground or a foot or
two up in small bushes; in either case the nest is usually
well concealed from view. There is a great difference in
the temperaments of individual birds of the same species.
One pair of Field Sparrows may perch on the top of a bush

Fig. 150. CLEANING THE NEST.

and chirp excitedly as long as an intruder is in sight, while another may quiet down in a very few moments and carry on their household duties as though they were alone. The birds shown in the accompanying pictures belonged to the latter class.

The nest, or what was later to be the nest, was discovered almost as the first straw was laid. During two hours following the discovery the nest grew wonderfully. The fe-

---

175

Fig. 151.   FIELD SPARROW.

male was the carpenter, her mate's part consisting of bringing part of the material. Both birds would usually depart together, but she always returned first and had her grasses wound into place and was ready to take his as soon as he appeared.

In the course of three weeks, three of the four eggs that she had laid, hatched. When the young were six days old, several pictures were taken of scenes at the nest. As in the case of the Chipping Sparrows no attempt at concealment was made; the camera was within three feet of the nest and I was seated on the ground just back of it. The birds paid scarcely any attention to me and were back at the nest in less than ten minutes after I had things in readiness for them. Ants, spiders and plant lice formed the bulk of the

food that was brought, although, occasionally a caterpillar
or a hard-shelled beetle would be brought in. Nearly all
their food was gathered from the ground, in fact many
times they would have pieces of grass also in their beaks,
that they had accidentally pulled up while seizing the insects.

Fig. 152. YOUNG FIELD SPARROWS.

On the twelfth day after the eggs hatched, the nest was
empty; the young were near by for the parents were anxiously calling. but we were able to find but two of them.

Grasshopper Sparrow.

This is one of the most inconspicuous of all sparrows.
The bird itself is of a rather shy nature and seldom allows
one to approach sufficiently near to study it in detail without the aid of a good field glass. Its song is just a weak
insect-like chirping or rather buzzing, a sound that would es-

From a painting

RUBY-THR. HUMMING BIRD

GOLDFINCH

From a painting

cape the notice of probably ninety-five out of a hundred persons. They make their homes on the ground in fields and pastures. When singing you can usually locate them on a stone wall, fence post or some little elevation in the middle of the field.

The continued presence of a pair of "Grasshoppers" in a field that I often crossed, finally tempted me to try and find their nest. A large stone in the middle of the field furnished a lookout perch for the male bird. He commenced chirping as soon as I climbed the wall and in a few moments his mate appeared on the rock too; it was impossible to tell from which direction she came as she was wholly concealed by the tall grass when she ran from the nest. Attempts on several days. to start her from the nest, failed because of the vigilance of the guard. until I almost despaired of finding it. One morning I crept carefully up to the wall and watched. without being seen, for over an hour. At last I was rewarded by seeing a sparrow-like bird fly from the grass. across the fields. Another wait of a half hour and she returned, first alighting on the rock beside the male and then. as she had no idea anyone was watching, she flew about fifty yards away and dropped into the grass at the same point she had risen from.

I got quickly over the wall and rushed to the spot; as the watchman had no time to warn her. she flushed from the nest within ten feet of me. It contained five pretty, white, spotted eggs in a little grass cup well arched over on the southern side so as to always be shaded within.

Daily visits were now paid, and the habits of the female gradually underwent a change as the eggs advanced in incubation, until she would allow me to reach a point where I could look in and see her. The next time, I took the camera already set on a short tripod. In order not to startle her too suddenly, I walked slowly by the nest several times, as though I did not see her, pausing a little longer each

Fig. 153. GRASSHOPPER SPARROW.

time when in front of the nest. But as soon as I brought the camera in view she was off like a flash and the trials were over for that day.

Several more trials on succeeding days got her a little used to the machine and one day I was able to get focussed, draw the slide from the holder and give an exposure of two seconds, the result of which is shown in the picture of her sitting on the nest Her brown eyes twinkled with excite- ment and anxiety but she kept her place and I quietly re- moved the camera and left her. The eggs hatched the next day but I troubled her no more as I could not spare more time for pictures of her, and I doubt if it would have been possible to have gotten them.

THE IMPOSTOR.

A happy pair of Maryland Yellow-throats selected as a place in which to build their house, a spot on the bank of a tiny brook. The male Yellow-throat was a beautiful bird, a gentlebird of leisure and fashion, he had a hand, or at least a voice, in all that went on in the little bird community in which he dwelt. He tried to settle all disputes that arose among the other birds, his notes of protest were loudest if anyones home was raided or disturbed by bird, mammal or man and he was the watchman of the village, his long, rattling alarm ringing out if any form of danger appeared.

He flashed here, there and everywhere, his beady eyes twinkling in their black mask as he peered from the under- brush, ever and anon he darted to the top of some shrub and his loud, clear "witchery-witchery-witchery" would ring out above the songs of other birds. He encouraged his mate to work her hardest at building their little cup-shaped home, but he did not assist her in any other way. The nest was made of grasses and strips of bark; it was set among the weeds so that the bottom just touched the ground. The in- side was very deep, as is customary among these birds,—so deep that the sitting bird was entirely below the rim.

Fig. 154. YELLOW-THROAT RETURNING TO NEST.

Fig. 155. NEST OF MARYLAND YELLOW-THROAT.

One morning a handsome little egg appeared in the nest, —delicate, white, spotted chiefly about the large end. The next morning another similar one lay beside it. At some time during that day the imposter appeared, a Cowbird. As Mrs. Yellow-throat was not at home and the gallant sire was having an argument with some of his neighbors, she settled comfortably on the top of the little nest and when she left, there were three eggs, one much larger than the others and more thickly spotted.

No one can tell the feelings of a little bird when it finds

a spurious egg in its nest. Birds, except in unusual instances, cannot count, but they must recognize the difference in sizes between the eggs. Usually they accept the odd one without protest but instances often occur when a little bird, wiser than others of her kind, rolls the undesired egg out of the nest or builds another bottom to her nest, sacrificing her own eggs with the one of the Cowbird.

Fig. 156.   YELLOW-THROAT ON NEST.

In this instance, the little Yellow-throat laid two more eggs of her own and the nest would hold no more. As usual, the Cowbird egg, probably because it is larger and receives more warmth from the sitting bird, hatched a day before the smaller eggs. I passed by the nest and watched the progress of the young nearly every morning. Male and female Yellow-throat were very busy feeding the little birds; the young Cowbird, because of his larger size and much larger appetite, received food twice to every once for the rightful occupants of the nest. Young Maryland Yellow-

throats are much stronger and more active than the young
of most other warblers, so that all four of them were able to
stand the crowding and pushing of the young Cowbird. In
many instances, especially when nests are located above
ground, the little birds that really belong there are crowded
out or else suffocated.

Fig. 157. *He started in alarm as he heard the click of the
camera shutter.*

My plans for pictures at this nest were wholly upset.
The day before I expected them to leave the nest, I appeared ready to do business. The four little Yellow-throats
and one large Cowbird were all in the nest but so crowded
they scarce could move. The tent was placed in position
and the camera carefully focussed. At the last moment I
reached out to remove an offending blade of grass that
would have appeared out of focus in a picture. Like a flash,

four little Yellow-throats scuttled away in four directions through the weeds. leaving their clumsy foster-brother in the nest. I caught just one of the little sprites but he proved unmanageable so that I had to let him go and confine my photographic attempts to the Cowbird.

Fig. 158. *A male Yellow-throat feeding a young Cowbird bigger than itself.*

He was perched on a branch in front of the camera and I waited for developments. The two adult Yellow-throats evidently talked the matter over and decided that she should look after her four. sprightly offspring. while he would take care of the larger. helpless member of the family. Sir Yellow-throat coaxed and he coaxed and scolded and scolded trying to make the young Cowbird leave the perch; he even tried to knock him off as he flew past. but the stolid youngster would not budge. He just opened his mouth to its fullest extent and begged loudly for something to eat; he cared not nor thought of danger,—just of his appetite.

The Yellow-throat finally concluded that it was useless to threaten, persuade or reason with such a young one and started searching for something with which to quiet it. He finally brought a green worm and, with many misgivings and false starts, hopped out on the branch where the large baby-bird stood flapping his wings and coaxing. Birds can move very quickly but I have never seen one jump as suddenly as Yellow-throat did when the shutter clicked. Before the picture was taken, which happened in one one-hundredth part of a second, he had made a complete beat of his wings as is clearly shown in the photograph. As no harm had come to him at the first shot, he was not as wary when he approached the second time, and I secured him on the plate without motion.

For a month afterward, that little Cowbird was still depending upon its small step-father, following him everywhere, always fluttering its wings and begging for more, more, more.

Fig. 159. NEST OF RED-EYED VIREO.

SWINGING HOMES.

Red-eyed Vireo

Bringing with them the good cheer of the south, Red-eyed Vireos return to northern United States about the middle of May. They are the most abundant of the vireos and are also the most persistent songsters that we have. From morn until night, song after song pours from their tireless throats until at times, especially when one is listening to a new or unusual song of some other bird, it becomes very irritating. The vireo song is a rather lazily whistled repetition of the word vireo with varying accents and modulations. It is a song that readily lends itself for the imaginative person to substitute numerous words and sentences; delivered in an intermittent, rambling, recitative manner that has given it the local name of "preacher-bird".

Vireos are among the most useful protectors of the foliage,—always busy; most birds stop work and raise the head to deliver their song but with this species, work and song go hand in hand, even though he be hanging head-down looking over the under surface of the leaves.

Some of my pleasantest hours among birds were passed at the home of a pair of Red-eyed Vireos, the one shown in the accompanying illustrations. These birds had chosen for their summer residences one of the prettiest places ever selected by a pair of vireos It was in a pleasant piece of woods overlooking a beautiful lake. Not only were their natural surroundings pleasant, but they had congenial neighbors on every side, a fact that added greatly to my pleasure.

While sitting within my photographic tent, beside this nest, I could, with my glasses, see all that happened at the home of a pair of Redstarts about three hundred feet away. About forty feet distant, in the vertical face of a gravel pit, was the entrance to a tunnel leading to the home of a pair of kingfishers. And within six feet of the edge of the

Fig. 160. VIREO ON NEST.

No'e that the rim of the basket is low on the right side so that the bird can sit comfortably.

tent was the nest of an Ovenbird, containing four eggs. These last birds did not get used to me for a long time and scolded a great deal. I imagine that some chipmunks living in a stump a short distance away could have thrown some light on the disappearance of the Ovenbird eggs, that took place before I made a second visit.

A little farther off, out of sight but still within stone's throw, were nests of Wood Thrush Catbird, Thrasher, Towhee. Veery. Prairie and Chestnut-sided Warblers and Indigo Bunting But let us return to the vireo nest. When I found it, the nest contained four eggs that were evidently well incubated, for the vireo was sitting very closely.

This nest was very strongly built of strips of bark, plant fibres and grasses woven into a compact basket that swung from a crotch of a young chestnut shoot. The side opposite the crotch was lower than the others, allowing the vireo to sit in a comfortable position instead of doubled up as is the bird on the other nest shown. But one picture was taken on the day the nest was found, the one showing the four eggs. Three days later the eggs had hatched.

On the morning that the little birds were five days old, we again visited the nest carrying camera and tent. As we approached, we saw that the mother bird was brooding her young and that her mate was standing on the edge of the nest beside her. At no time while we had the camera in position did both birds come to the nest at the same time, although frequently one stood just out of range while its mate was busy feeding the babies

The young were fed with clock-like precision beginning within ten minutes from the time the tent was set up. The longest period of waiting between visits was ten minutes and the shortest, two minutes. They were fed chiefly upon various worms and caterpillars, with an occasional dragon-fly or moth. The picture showing the male vireo with his bill thrust down the throat of one little fellow illustrates a number of interesting points. First —Birds do not simply

drop food into the mouths of their little ones but thrust it
far down the throat. Second:—Notice that the head of
the one being fed is raised higher than the others. The
more hungry a little bird is, the higher it will reach, a fact
that insures their being fed in rotation. The little fellow

Fig. 161. *On one occasion the male brought a large dragon-
fly, carefully divested of wings and all but one leg.*

in front is much smaller and a day or two younger than the
other two (the fourth egg did not hatch), but when the
next morsel was brought his wide-open, appealing mouth
was raised above that of his brothers and sisters. Third:—
Notice the motion of the head of the young bird on the

Fig. 162. *Food is thrust well down the throats of the little ones.*

right. In this case the whole head, as shown by the lower mandible. was oscillating about the upper mandible as an axis. It is this rapid motion of little birds that spoils many a photograph.

On one occasion, the male vireo brought a large dragon-

Fig. 163 *He moved too quickly for the camera shutter this time.*

fly which he carefully prepared for nestling-food by divesting it of wings and all but one leg. He then walked along the branch and thrust it headfirst down the throat of one of his children, leaving fully an inch of the body sticking out of the little fellows mouth. I had supposed that he would surely divide the fly into a portion for each and was greatly astonished to see him feed such a large morsel to such a small bird. The contortions of the little fellow, as he slowly but surely swallowed the dragonfly, were painful to watch; it took about four minutes for it to entirely disappear from view. For fifteen minutes this little bird lay quietly in the bottom of the nest, at the end of which time he again bobbed up, as hungry as ever.

Fig. 164. VIREO ENTERING NEST.

I show two views of another nest located in a little oak. This nest is of the ordinary type, with a high rim all around so that the sitting bird has to have her tail erect. The black-bordered superciliary and maxillary lines on the bird entering the nest from the rear, give its face a very peculiar

From a painting

BALTIMORE ORIOLE

From a painting

FLICKER

Fig. 165.   RED-EYED VIREO.

appearance, almost as though it were equipped with auto-mobile goggles.

This last nest was in a very ill-chosen location. When these pictures were made, at which time the nest contained eggs, the bottom of the structure was less than six inches from the ground. By the time the eggs had hatched and the young were a week old, the nest touched the ground. Two days later it was empty; some marauding animal had made away with the little birds and perhaps captured the mother too, for I did not see her again although the male was in the neighborhood for several weeks.

13

THE VIREO

Bertha A. Joslin.

"Dear me dear me, hear me. hear me."
   What's the matter pray?
Clatter, clatter; chatter. chatter,
   All the livelong day.
Up among the bloom and leaf.
   Peeping out from underneath,
Little bird so pretty, O,
   Don't you ever stop to breathe,
Darling little Vireo?

Trees that screen it, dainty greenlet.
   Never screen its song.
"What so happy, O, as the Vireo?"
   Ringeth loud and long.
"What so cheery, O, as the Vireo,
   What so jolly, O, sweet,
What so merry, O, as the Vireo?"
   All the leaves repeat.

If rain doth spatter, thunder clatter,
   Still for a bit I'll be.
But the sun's behind it, I never mind it,
   Safe up in my tree
It does not matter. the clouds will scatter,
   So I rest myself a wee,
Then clatter, clatter, chatter, chatter,
   Over lawn and lea.
"Hear me. the Vireo, all so merry, O."
   Bubbling in my tree

Yellow-throated Vireo.

The home of the Yellow-throated Vireo is usually swung from the fork of a branch ranging from ten to forty feet above ground, while that of the Red-eyed species is usually found less than ten feet up. The nests of the two species are constructed so nearly alike that they cannot be distinguished from one another positively, but the eggs of the present species have a very few, small reddish-brown spots while those on the eggs of Red-eye are black.

The song of the Yellow-throated Vireo is very different from that of the Red-eye, although anyone would readily recognize it as that of some sort of a vireo. It is lower in pitch, the tones are not clear, there being a distinct undertone the song is more deliberate and the pauses much longer; he is very apt, too to break off into a chatter in the midst of his song

The two young vireos of this species, that are pictured here, were so unfortunate as to be blown from their cradle, swinging forty feet up in an oak tree, by a very high wind They happened to fall without injury and were so good as to allow us to take their portraits We also made several of the mother bird feeding these, but none of them came out satisfactorily because of the gale that caused tent and camera to vibrate and nearly blew the feathers off the birds. It is my only attempt at picturing these birds, but good results should be secured under favorable circumstances, as both the young and the adults were very tractable.

California Bush-tit

These little birds rank next to the hummingbirds as being the smallest birds found in our country. Diminutive as they are, being but four inches long, half of which length is comprised in the tail, they fashion beautiful hanging nests that are bulky enough for birds four times their size These purse-shaped nests, constructed of mosses, lichens, plant fibres and feathers, and with the entrance a little hole on one side near the top, vary in length from six to sixteen inches

Fig. 166.   BUSH-TIT AND NEST.

Fig. 167. NEST OF BUSH-TIT.

In southern California, the birds are quite common but, because of their small size are not as apt to be noticed as are the nests that hang conspicuously from the branches of many of the oaks. Nimble as our chickadees are, their acrobatic feats are more than equaled by those of this tiny creature which delights in whirling about tiny branches or dropping from one to another while upside down.

Their diminutive forms and gray color make them very inconspicuous and their weak voices are not likely to call attention to them as they industriously search thickets and foliage of large trees, ridding them of quantities of little pests.

Fig. 168. *Female Golden-winged Warbler returning to her nest. She was very tame and I made 8 negatives of her but unfortunately all except this were "light-struck."*

199

THE GLEANERS.

Birds are the natural conservators of our trees. One of their chief offices is the destruction of insects whose ravages destroy the foliage or eat the very hearts out of our shade and forest trees.

Chief among the gleaners of the foliage are the warblers

Fig. 169. *Black and White Warbler entering its nest.*

and vireos; they search the trunks of trees, peer in all the crevices and hang from the tips of the slenderest branches, devouring insect-eggs, worms, caterpillars, larvae and fully developed flies or moths. I have been very fortunate in being able to secure photographic histories of a number of these gleaners.

BLACK AND WHITE WARBLER.

Woodpeckers are very expert at climbing up trees; Nuthatches are equally expert at clambering down. Black

Fig. 170. BLACK AND WHITE WARBLER ON HER NEST.

and White Warblers or Black and White Creepers, as they were formerly called, are more versatile and agile than either; they can climb in any position with the greatest of ease. In this respect, their habits are so different from most warblers, that early naturalists were inclined to class them in a separate family.

After hearing the long-drawn, wiry song of a Black and White Warbler coming from about the same spot for several consecutive mornings, I decided to investigate Climbing over the wall, I went in the direction of his voice and soon found him climbing nimbly about in a young chestnut tree in search of his breakfast Every few moments the little climber would pause, lift his head and sing out his unmusical notes. I was not particularly interested in the male bird at this time, but I knew that somewhere near him I would find his mate and that having located her, it would be a comparatively easy matter to find their nest.

I soon discovered her in a tree beyond her mate, and was delighted to see that she had a long shred of bark in her beak As usual with birds of this species, she was very careful and wanted to make sure that no one should see her building the nest I kept perfectly still for fully fifteen minutes before she went to its site, which proved to be at the base, on the opposite side, of the very stump behind which I was concealed. As these warblers are very apt to desert a nest if they know it to be discovered, I went quietly away without even looking at it.

The next time I saw the nest it contained one dainty little warbler egg and a larger one of a Cowbird; the latter egg was removed because it would have either prevented the warbler from laying her full number of eggs in the nest or else, when hatched, the young Cowbird would probably have crowded some of the smaller birds to death I saw neither of the warblers on that morning and feared that they might have already deserted the nest because of the imposition

Fig. 171. *She always returned the same way,—down a dead limb to a tiny twig; dropping from the latter to her doorway.*

of the Cowbird. A week later I returned and, when at a
distance of about ten feet, I could see her little bead-like
eyes and black and white striped face. The nest was sunk
among the leaves at the base of the stump and was well
arched over so that it was very difficult to see even when the
exact location was known. She sat perfectly still and I
approached very, very slowly carrying a camera, already

Fig. 172. *Four of the five little ones; the other could not be
found.*

set on its tripod, before me. I managed to plant it so that
the lens was but three feet from her without causing her to
leave. Then still more slowly, at the same time trying to
reassure her with bird-like chirps (that perhaps did not
sound much like a bird), I leaned forward and removed
some objectionable grasses that were between the lens and
her and finally lifted the arch a trifle so that she could be
seen to better advantage. She was frightened, for she

breathed faster than normal but she made no move to get away and even opened her bill as though to pick my fingers when I touched the nest.

Her confidence and courage were amazing, considering that it was the first formal visit I had made. With a small stop in the lens, I made two pictures of her as she sat on the nest. As I did not wish to frighten her away, I simply

Fig. 173. *I managed to keep two of them on a twig long enough to get his picture, feeding them; they were so active that this was almost a hopeless task.*

wound my coat and focussing cloth about the tripod legs and went to another part of the woods. leaving the camera there. As I had hoped, when I returned an hour later she had left her nest, which, I now saw, held five eggs, and gone after food. So I stretched myself on the ground with just my head and shoulders concealed under the small tent formed by the covered tripod legs and, with bulb in hand, awaited her return.

It was a very clear, sunny day in the middle of June. The sun's rays were very warm, in fact I never before realized that they were so red hot. In spite of the discomfort, I had to laugh as I likened myself to a turkey in the oven; the worst of it was I was being baked only on one side; I could not turn over because my warbler had returned and was watching me closely before going to the nest. At the end of about fifteen minutes, by which time I was "well

Fig. 174. *They moved so rapidly that the picture is blurred although it was made in 1-200 of a second.*

done", she got in just the position I wanted and I snapped the shutter. One such roasting as that was sufficient so I gathered my outfit and retreated.

It was fortunate that I took the pictures as I did, for when I next returned with my whole battery of cameras and tent, I found that I was a day too late. I no sooner touched the nest than the little black and white fellows slid out in all directions. I think that, possibly with the exception of some little Maryland Yellow-throats, they were the liveliest lot of little birds I have ever handled. I never needed an

Fig. 175. *The male bird even went into the valise to feed the little ones. Notice that he is now standing on the edge and one young is inside.*

assistant as much as I did at just that time. After much running, dodging and climbing I managed to corral four of them but I could find no trace of the fifth; its mother had led it away and left the father bird to look out for the ones I had.

If human children would obey their parents as beautifully as these little birds did, we would have a perfect world. As soon as I got them perched on a branch he would tell them to get off,—and off they would go, every one of them, in four different directions. I did manage to get a few pictures but not the ones that I wanted most to secure. The male warbler was the most courageous little feathered mite

207

I have ever seen. He was everywhere almost at once, climbing all over my head, shoulders and hands, but never still for an instant. He pleaded so earnestly for me to let his little ones go, that I soon turned them loose.

CHESTNUT-SIDED WARBLER.

Both this species and the Black and White Warbler are about equally common, but the nests of the Chestnut-side are much more easily found. The birds are not as careful to avoid being seen and the nests are above ground so that they are often found without watching the owner. They are, however, located usually at the top of low bushes so they can be seen only below by removing the protecting leaves from above.

Fig. 176. CHESTNUT-SIDE ON NEST.

Fig. 177. *Male Chestnut-sided Warbler feeding one of its young; there are three in the nest but not in sight.*

209

They are among the easiest of birds to photograph while they are sitting upon the nest. Several times I have removed leaves from above the bird, put a camera in place and made photographs without disturbing her; they sometimes have allowed me also to gently stroke their back, without leaving the eggs. They seem to be very popular with that

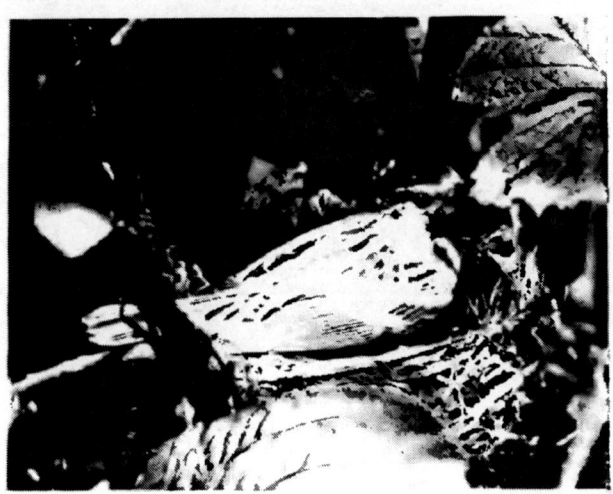

Fig. 178. *I advanced until the lens was within 2 feet of her and she half rose from the eggs.*

bird-parasite, the Cowbird, for about twenty-five per cent. of the nests found contain one or more eggs of this species.

Although Sir Chestnut-side leaves the task of making the nest almost wholly to his mate, he takes his turn at sitting on the eggs and, in almost every case that I have watched, does more than his share in feeding the little ones. With most birds that I have photographed, it has been the female that returned first after the battery of cameras was trained on the nest, but with Chestnut-sides it has always been the male which showed the way.

It was several years before I was able to secure any pictures of the parent birds feeding their little ones. Nearly

14

Fig. 179. *She jumped at the click of the shutter.*

Fig. 180. FEMALE CHESTNUT-SIDE.

Fig. 181.

every nest of this species that I located would be destroyed
in some manner before the eggs hatched or something would
take the little ones while they were very small. The fact
that most of the nests were in a locality where chipmunks
and grackles abounded was perhaps responsible for the
great destruction of eggs and young.

Prairie Warbler.

These beautiful little warblers are very locally distributed. They nest usually in small colonies, one of which happens to be on a certain side hill where I have succeeded in
making pictures of a great many species of birds. Each
male seems to have his own little section and also a favorite

Fig. 182. NEST OF PRAIRIE WARBLER.

lookout perch; many an exciting chase occurs when the head of some one household encroaches on the domains of another A flash of yellow and black is all that can be seen of the bewildering conflicts as they dash in and out among the underbrush until one finally returns to his perch singing his victory in the peculiar. rasping tones common to this species.

Their nests are quite difficult to find as they are, almost without exception. built at the tops of low shrubs, just where the leaves are the most dense As there are hundreds of bushes perfectly adapted to their needs it requires a long search to locate a nest. particularly because these warblers are so very careful not to disclose its hiding place. All my observations have brought me to the conclusion that Prairie Warblers are practical jokers. I, at least, have been made their victim on several occasions.

One day I saw one of the females with a bit of grass in her bill, so I sat down to watch and find out where she was going to put it. She knew that I had seen her so she chirped and scolded for a long time. being ably aided by her mate who appeared by her side at the first note of alarm. In a few minutes she took the nesting material into the thick top of a bush and soon flew out again without it. A few minutes later, the male also carried material to the same spot followed after awhile by the female with some strips of bark. I was sure that they must have a nest nearly completed to be working so industriously, so I went over to investigate. Imagine my surprise when I found not a shred of a nest there; they had carried their loads to the bush and dropped them on the ground apparently for the very purpose of fooling me. I have had other very similar experiences with these little warblers.

I show a few pictures obtained at a nest located in a young walnut tree. It is a typical nest, composed chiefly of plant fibres, a few grasses and shreds of bark. While

Fig. 183. MALE PRAIRIE WARBLER.

215

Fig. 184. FEMALE PRAIRIE WARBLER.

the female was sitting, both she and her mate were watchful. She always left the nest and glided away unseen if anyone approached. As soon as the eggs had hatched, the parents lost much of their fear and would feed the little birds even while we were watching.

When bringing food, they approached the nest cautiously, keeping near the ground where the swaying of the tops of the sweet ferns, that formed the lower strata of vegetation, showed their approach and soon a tremor of the walnut announced that they were almost at the goal. All manner of insects were included in their menu,—ants, aphids, flies, moths and even repulsive looking little worms such as one of the illustrations shows the male bird bringing.

Fig. 185.   NEST OF OVENBIRD.

Arched over so that one has to stoop low to look under and see the eggs.

The good fellowship that exists between birds can be judged by the number that nested in company with the Prairie Warblers, within a radius of one hundred yards. They included Indigo Buntings, Towhees, Veeries, Thrashers, Vireos, Black and White and Chestnut-sided Warblers, Field and Song Sparrows, a Chickadee. Bluebird and Scarlet Tanger. As a general thing they all lived very peaceably with only an occasional tilt that in no ways disturbed the social equilibrum of the bird community.

THE OVENBIRD.

In early morning, during spring and summer, the woodland resounds with the loud, vibrant songs of Ovenbirds,—"teacher-teacher-teacher- - - - - - -" repeated many times and giving the species the local name of "Teacher-bird". It is also very commonly known as the Golden-crowned Thrush because it has a dull, orange-yellow stripe on the crown and because the rest of the coloration is thrush-like. The reason for the name of Ovenbird is rather obscure to the beginner in bird study until he or she has discovered one of their nests.

One morning, as we approached a pretty bit of woodland, above the sweet voices of numerous other songsters, we heard the loud chanting of an Ovenbird. Ere the last notes of his ditty had been uttered, the song was taken up and continued by other Ovenbirds in distant parts of the woods. Usually nests of these birds are found by flushing the sitting bird, the present instance being the only one in which I ever discovered the nest of an Ovenbird before seeing the owner. We had barely entered the woods before I noticed a slight elevation of the leaves ahead of us. Instinctively the thought came to mind that it was a nest; approaching carefully, we stooped and looked under the arching top. Greatly disturbed by this undesired curiosity the owner, an Ovenbird of course, dashed out and from a branch close at hand scolded us roundly.

It was a fine type of the nest of this species; the top was strongly arched over, so much so that the eggs could barely be seen. Concluding that, as we had discovered the little oven so easily, others might do the same, we made a picture of the nest and eggs and then set the camera so as to get a picture of the returning bird, although the light in the shady woods was very poor for quick exposures. As soon as we were concealed within the tent the Ovenbird ceased her anxious chirping, hopped down on the ground

Fig. 186. OVENBIRD RETURNING TO NEST.

and apparently commenced to walk aimlessly about picking
up a bit of food here and there.

The Ovenbird walks, not hops, very daintily; Mr. Ernest
Seton Thompson has very aptly termed the bird "A Pretty
Pedestrian". Every circuit brought her closer to her little
oven-like home, until at last she hopped on a twig just
over the arch, and within the scope of the lens. A sharp
click and one more bird had been photographically shot.
We were fortunate to have taken these pictures as we did,
for two days later a slight hollow in the ground was the

only sign of where the nest had been. Whether its disappearance was due to a two or a four-footed animal could not be surmised as red squirrels were abundant in the woods and people were constantly crossing.

The finding of another nest, a few days later, yielded one more picture of an Ovenbird just entering her "oven".

Fig. 187. OVENBIRD ENTERING NEST.

This nest too was destroyed, presumably by chipmunks, before the eggs had hatched.

YELLOW WARBLER.

The Yellow Warbler or "Summer Yellowbird" is a beautiful, little, golden sprite that we are sure to find flitting about in clumps of willows or alders that overhang almost any brook. We often find them, too, in orchards for they take very kindly to civilization. Its song is a simple little ditty, "cher-wee, cher-wee, swee- swee", very similar to that of the Chestnut-sided Warbler and the Redstart.

Yellow Warblers weave very pretty little homes of plant

Fig. 188.   NEST OF YELLOW WARBLER.

fibres in crotches of bushes, not very high above ground. One of the most beautiful nests that I ever have seen was made by a pair of these birds. It was located near a cotton mill and the outside of the nests was composed entirely of snow-white cotton, the inside being lined with the usual horsehair.

As far as my observations go, these warblers seem to be imposed on by Cowbirds more than any other unless it be the Chestnut-sided. The percentage of nests containing these obnoxious eggs is quite large and the resulting mortality due to the over-crowding of the nest, is also quite large among the little Yellow Warblers.

Fig. 189. NEST OF KINGFISHER.

Fig. 189. KINGFISHER WITH MULLET FOR ITS YOUNG.

FISHER-BIRDS.

Belted Kingfisher.

One June day, a friend, while roaming about on the edge of some woods, suddenly felt the earth giving way beneath his feet and sprang to one side just in time, as he soon discovered, to avoid crushing a family of young kingfishers. Probably the old birds had misjudged the thickness of the earth and made the roof of their house too high, for examination showed that less than half an inch of earth separated the chamber from the outer world.

My friend was very enthusiastic in his description of how handsome the little fellows were and it took little urging to induce me to accompany him to the scene the next day. I found that he had repaired the break in their home by placing a large flat stone over it, so that the place was much more secure than before it had been broken into. The entrance to the home, that is the proper one, was located in the side of a gravel pit about six feet from the chamber where the little kingfishers lay. We decided, before opening the nest again, to try and get a few views of the adult entering; as there were several roots projecting from the earth within a few inches of the opening, I expected that the birds would alight on one of these before entering.

The camera was placed on a rock five feet from the opening, and carefully covered; the shutter was to be operated with a thread running to a clump of bushes about twenty yards distant. A few minutes after we had comfortably seated oureslves in our ambush, a warning rattle was heard from the bed of the brook, to be repeated a moment later from close at hand. Guided by the sound. we soon located the mother kingfisher perched on the lower limb of an oak and. as we had expected. she held a small fish in her beak.

She had not seen us come and was apparently very much surprised to find a new, curious. bulky object (the camera) so near her home. Surely this had not been there when

Fig. 190.   ADULT KINGFISHER ENTERING NESTING TUNNEL.

she came last. She watched it long and very closely, nervously flirting her tail just as sandpipers are wont to do. At least once she changed the position of the fish she carried by tossing it a few inches in the air and catching it again. Having satisfied herself that the camera was not alive, after a great deal of scolding, she flew directly to the entrance

Fig. 191. *The bank cut away to show the little "fishers" at the end of the tunnel.*

to her home; greatly to my surprise, she alighted neither on the roots nor on the edge of the hole, but seemed to dash right in without a pause. Her departure was almost as rapid; she backed out the length of the tunnel and, just as her tail appeared at the opening, whirled about and was off in a flash.

During half a dozen visits that she made, she entered and left in the same manner: as I was not prepared to make moving pictures, the best I could do was to "get her" backing out, just as she started to turn about. The bird shown

15

in one of the illustrations, with a mullet in its bill, was more considerate for she lit on a stick thrust into the bank for that purpose and allowed Mr. R. H. Beebe to take several pictures of her.

Young kingfishers are very comical birds both in appearance and in actions. At an early age, they are entirely cov-

Fig. 192. *Little Kingfishers are very "spiney" or pin-feathery during the early stages of their life.*

ered with coarse pin-feathers, giving them a bristly appearance like little porcupines. They remain in the nest about three weeks at the end of which time they closely resemble their parents in plumage. Although six or seven of them have to occupy rather cramped quarters in their home, it does not seem to develop brotherly love to any great extent. They always seem to be biting at one another. On one occasion when I had seven of them side by side on a rail, a youngster on one end grabbed the fellow next to him by the wing; this one seized the next and so on along the whole row, the seven of them finally going to the ground in a connected tangle. Undoubtedly, their rough actions hasten their development by bursting the casing of the pin-feathers sooner than they would unaided, and it may be that this is the purpose of their roughness.

The tunnel that leads to the nest is just large enough for one bird and gives him no room to turn around. When the young get so they can walk, even though clumsily, they often meet their parent at the door way,—at least one does,

Fig. 193. SEVEN LITTLE KINGS.

with the others crowding in a line behind. Before feeding even the first one, the parent will usually force them all back into the enlarged chamber. This walking in single file, usually in step, forward and backward often gets them into the habit of moving in unison when they are removed from the nest. It is a most comical sight to see seven, frizzly-headed birds deliberately take three or four steps forward, backward or sidewise, as the case may be, in

Fig. 194. YOUTHFUL FISHERBIRDS.

Fig. 195. *They often grabbed and bit at one another.*

perfect lock step as though controlled by one mind or master.

Little kingfishers do not seem to know fear until after they have made their first flight. Housed in as they are, they have no chance to see what goes on in the outer world and, if a man happens along, takes them out of their nest and groups them on a rock or branch, they take it just as a matter of course, as though it were something that ought to happen. After they have made their maiden flight, however, they object to being handled and will sometimes bite savagely.

Their parents feed them for more than a week after they leave the nest, but all the time their wings are getting stronger and stronger so that soon they can hover over the water and pounce on little fish, just as their parents do.

The food of kingfishers consists wholly of small fish up
to four inches in length. They are very persistent in their
fishing, as much so as the man that often sits with his line
dangling in the water for several hours without getting a
bite. I once watched one of these birds, that happened to

Fig. 196. A HANDSOME FAMILY.

be perched where I could see it from my blind as I was
taking pictures at a Vireo nest, and for two hours it sat perfectly still, watching the water below it, before it got a
chance to plunge and then it missed the fish. However, they
make a very fair percentage of successful strikes, always
catching their prey between the opened mandibles.

Osprey; Fish Hawk.

The Osprey is probably the most widely distributed of all birds; it is found at the proper season in nearly every country on the globe. It is a very inoffensive bird, living exclusively upon a fish diet. While essentially a salt water bird it is often found about the larger lakes, especially during migrations.

Ospreys are strongly protected both by law and public sentiment in most places where they are common and breed but as soon as they wander from their regular abiding places they put their lives in jeopardy for uneducated farmers consider all large birds as "hen-hawks" and certain classes of hunters take a shot at everything of size that comes within range.

The same birds return to the same breeding grounds, and to the same nests, each year. The nests are normally placed among the upper branches of dead trees; they are large structures when first built and as they are used and added to each succeeding year. they soon become very bulky, I have seen a number that would more than fill an ordinary tip-cart. Osprey eggs are usually regarded as the most beautifully marked of all hawks,—a rich, creamy ground color, covered with bright blotches of reddish-brown and umber.

It is very interesting to watch Ospreys at their fishing grounds,—to see them sailing smoothly along on motionless pinions or wending their way homeward with a steady flapping, bearing their catch to waiting, little Ospreys When on the lookout for fish. they usually sweep along at an elevation of perhaps one hundred feet above water. As soon as one is sighted in a favorable position, the Osprey hovers for a few moments, with wings rapidly beating the air and, if his quarry does not take alarm. quickly folds his wings

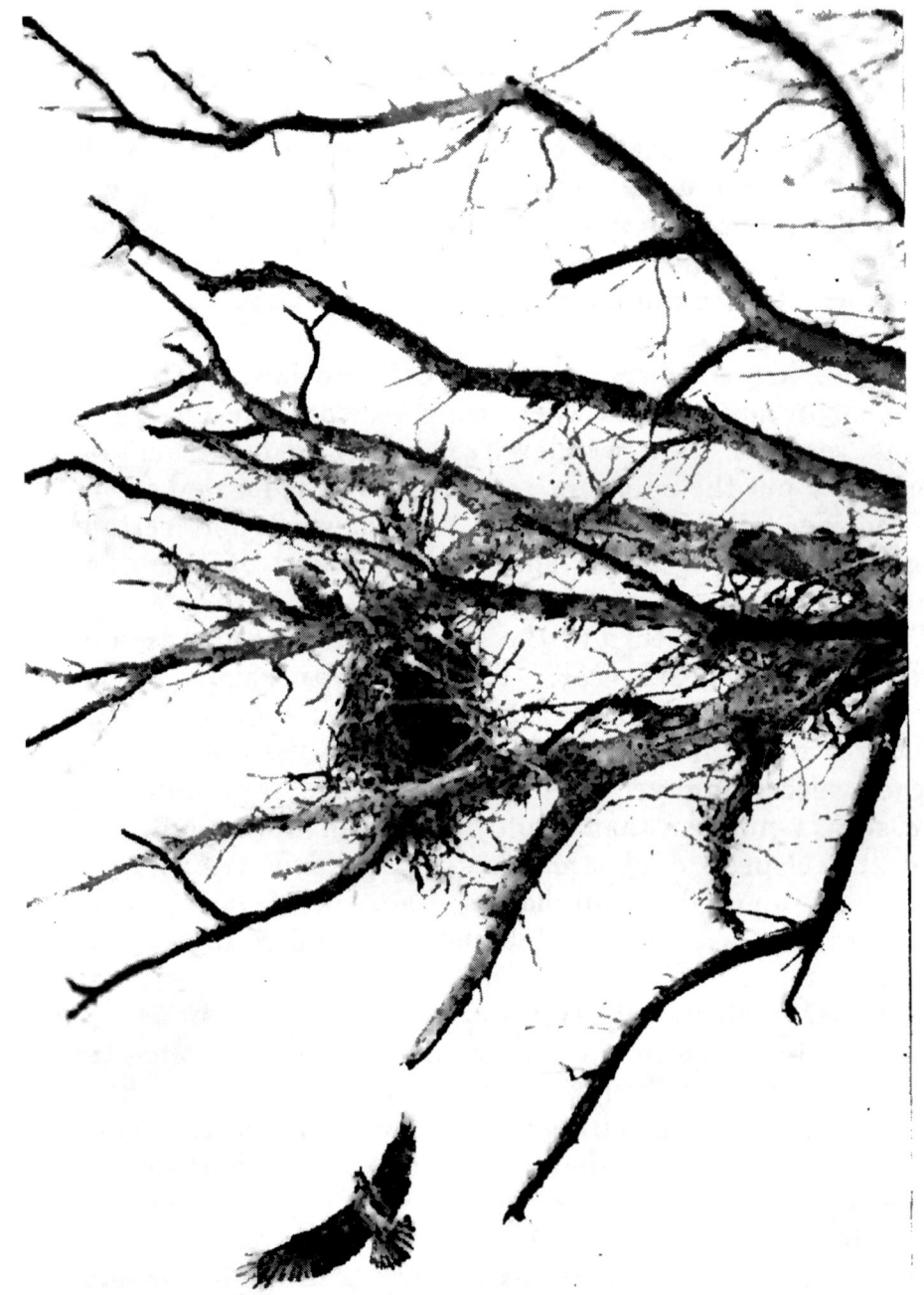

Fig. 197. OSPREY RETURNING TO NEST.
Note its mate perched back of nest.

Fig. 198   BOTH BIRDS CIRCLED OVERHEAD.

and shoots downward, headfirst, just before striking the water, the long legs are thrown forward so that the sharp talons reach even in front of his head,—he accomplishes the remarkable feat of diving into the water both headfirst and feet-first at one and the same time. The average success of Fish Hawks at their trade, seems to be about one catch to three misses. They will catch any kind of fish that swim near the surface.—fish weighing, usually. from a half pound to two or three pounds.

Fig. 199.   OSPREY LEAVING NEST.

Twice in one day, I witnessed a scene in bird-dom that is rarely observed,—that of an eagle pursuing an Osprey. This act was first noted by Audubon and has been copied widely from his writings, but few have had the opportunity of actually seeing it. Near Lynnhaven Inlet on the coast of Virginia, Bald Eagles were very plentiful as also were Ospreys. The latter caught most of their fish out of the nets that were set at frequent intervals by fishermen. The eagles fed largely upon dead fish that washed ashore, the same as did the buzzards, but often they, too, went fishing in the weirs.

I had located an Osprey nest, containing young, about two hundred yards from the beach; standing at the foot of this tree I could, at one time, count sixteen eagles in sight. To decide whether the Ospreys and eagles were on friendly terms, I spent the greater part of a day watching them. Unfortunately, as it was a ten mile walk from my stopping place, I did not have my graflex with me.

One of the Ospreys, bearing a fish in its talons, came to the nest about every half hour. Although several eagles were perched on some of the dead trees, which were half covered by the drifting sands, within a hundred yards of the nest, they did not attempt to molest the smaller bird except in two instances; they did, however, all watch the incoming hawks with the greatest of interest.

On one occasion, perhaps in a spirit of bravado for, with food so plenty there was no excuse for marauding, a young, very dark, Bald Eagle, uttering a single shrill whistle, flew to meet a returning Osprey. Evidently the same thing had happened before for the hawk immediately wheeled and started mounting skyward, uttering piercing, tremulous screams. With only an occasional flap of his huge wings, the eagle closely followed, ascending in wide spirals until both were nearly lost to view, even when viewed with powerful binoculars. I should judge that they were

Fig. 200. ABOUT TO ALIGHT.

fully two miles up when the hawk released his prey,—so high that I could not see what happened. but the eagle came swooping grandly to the perch he had left, bearing the prize, while the poor Osprey went out to the weirs for another one. Undoubtedly stolen fish tasted much sweeter to the eagle than if he had captured it himself, even though the latter course would have required but a fractional part of the energy he expended in mounting to the clouds.

On another occasion the same thing happened, but the Osprey released his prey before he had ascended half a mile. the eagle lazily reaching out one leg and grasping it as it fell past him. Eagles have wonderful control of themselves when in the air. I have seen one, that was attacked by crows from above it. repeatedly turn completely over in midair and present his talons toward his tormentors.

Ospreys nest not only in dead trees but on cliffs, on the ground. on the cross arms of telegraph poles and even on unused chimneys.

Fig. 201.   NEST OF SPOTTED SANDPIPER.

Sandpiper eggs are very handsome,—gray buff, blotched and specked with blackish-brown.

239

MY SANDPIPER FRIENDS.

We were destined to become friends. For years, as long ago as I can remember, these Spotted Sandpipers, or some of their ancestors, had frequented the shores of a tiny pond and had, each year, built their nests in some of the bordering fields. Likewise, as far back as my memory takes me, the fields surrounding this same little pond were included in one of my favorite and most frequent rambles. Each year, the first week in May, I have welcomed my sandpiper

Fig. 202. RETURNING TO HER NEST.

Fig. 203. *She stepped carefully up to the nest and fondled the eggs with her bill.*

friends on their return from the sunny south, have listened
to their fife-like notes as they chased one another about, or
have watched them skimming across the pond with the peculiar, tremulous flutter of the down-curved wings, characteristic of sandpipers.

By the end of May, they cease their play and settle down
to business. Having selected a suitable spot, the female
builds a nest,—not a very strenuous task, for she simply
squats in the grass and turns around a few times, thus form-
ing a hollow of the correct shape. Sometimes she will wind
a few grasses around the hollow but often she does not do
even that much.

One morning as I passed through a clearing in some
small pines near the pond, a bird fluttered from nearly
under my feet. A glance proved it to be a Spotted Sandpiper and another glance showed me that I had nearly trod
upon the four eggs upon which she had been sitting. She
tried her best to lead me away; apparently she was very
severely wounded for she limped with one leg, both wings
dragged on the ground and, every few steps, she would fall
over as though exhausted It was a very fine piece of act-
ing and would deceive anyone not accustomed to it (still
men who profess to be scientists say that birds and mammals have no intelligence; personally I believe that many
birds and many mammals have a higher degree of intelli
gence than some of those who claim everything is done by
instinct or imitation).

Although I had found a great many nests of these birds,
I was glad to locate this because I had never made photographs of them and this nest offered an excellent opportunity to do so. The eggs were handsomely marked, as is
usual with those of this species; they had little to conceal
them from view. except their coloration, which harmonized
so well with the surroundings that, at ten feet distance it
was almost impossible to pick them out.

Fig. 204. *She sat there as calmly as if I were miles away, though I could have reached out and touched her.*

As I have said, this nest was in a clearing where there was not a particle of shelter, not even a spear of grass to keep the sun's rays off at any time during the day. On exceedingly warm days, I used often to think of this bird, sitting there, panting, but faithful to her charges. Even worse to endure than the sun, was the rain. At that time, there occurred four days of the heaviest rainfall we had ever experienced and I was very doubtful about her being able to stand it. However when the sun shone on the morning of the fifth day, she slipped away from the nest, upon my approach, none the worse for her drenching. Only one who has been caught in the fields or woods, far from shelter, in a driving rain, can appreciate the hardships that birds have to undergo at such times.

Early one morning, I appeared with all my paraphernalia for picture making. She slid off the eggs as usual and flew down to the pond; she knew from experience that I would not be deceived so she never now tried to feign lameness. Just for an experiment, one morning later, I had a friend approach the nest first and she tried her best to decoy him away. Certainly this showed at least a ray of intelligence for, while she knew that I was aware of her nest and reasoned that it would be useless to try and deceive me, she tried it with everyone else.

I used a green umbrella-tent placed so that the front edge was about two feet from the eggs. This was covered with small pine branches, not to deceive the bird, but so as not to attract much notice should anyone come that way, as they frequently did. I soon had a camera focussed carefully on the eggs and was lying comfortably on the ground awaiting the return of my hostess. Presently I heard her approaching, her calls sounding plainer and plainer each time they were repeated. Finally she stood on a stone about twenty feet away, 'teetering' as sandpipers always do, and eying sharply the new addition to the landscape

Everything was perfectly still and there seemed to be no signs of life about, so she stepped from her elevation and approached, slowly, uncertainly and with many pauses to look anxiously about her. She made a complete circuit of the tent three times, often brushing against its sides and passing within six inches of the small peek-hole through which I was breathlessly watching. Finally she stopped

Fig. 205. *She stepped carefully between the eggs and settled down.*

Fig. 206. *She kept a sharp watch of the great glass eyes that stared so steadily at her, only three feet away.*

at her nest, gently touched one of the eggs with her bill and then, suddenly catching sight of the great camera-eye staring at her, quickly jumped back. Approaching even more cautiously, she ran right across the eggs and whirled about quickly to see if anything happened. The next time she fondled all the eggs and at last was contentedly settled upon them.

The click of the shutter the first few exposures, startled her a trifle but she very quickly got accustomed to it and paid no attention to the tent or anything that went on within

Fig. 207. *From time to time she half arose and carefully treaded the eggs over.*

it. I even opened a large flap in the front of the tent, stuck my head out and watched her from a distance of less than twenty-four inches, without frightening her off the nest. I often wondered what she thought of the new conditions and what wonderful tales she told her mate when she joined him at the edge of the pond. I think she must have concluded that I was harmless, had built a large green nest near hers and was as much entitled to live there as she was.

Invariably when returning to the nest, after a short absence, she would feel of the eggs with her bill, carefully turn them over. then cautiously step on or between them and settle down to her task. When sitting, her wings were drooped so as to rest on the ground and her head was drawn well back on her shoulders. She seemed to be interested in all that transpired about her. watching the small birds as they flitted through the pines and twisting her head in all manner of positions to watch others as they flew overhead.

Three times. while I watched. danger threatened her home, but she met it bravely and in the best manner to fit the occasion. Once she saw a man coming through the trees before I had heard his approach; her feathers drew closer to her sides and she became as motionless as the stone beside her. When he was within about twenty yards she slipped quietly off the nest, sneaked through the scanty grass to a distance of about thirty feet and hid behind a larger stone. The man passed without even noticing my tent and the sandpiper came leisurely back. stopping several times to pick up insects.

The next time we were disturbed. we did not escape so easily. A man approached from the rear so quickly that there was no time for her to hide; he came lumbering through the pines. going right over any bushes that were in his path. I was forced to step out of the tent and stop him for fear he would go right over it. He started back as though he had seen a ghost, with a "Waall I swan! I never seen yer!" I explained that I was making photographs, but did not say what of, and he went his way without seeing the nest nor the bird that was running off with trailing wings.

The third danger might have been serious had I not been there, but believe she would have pulled through all right. She was sitting quietly on her eggs. tending strictly to business, when I suddenly saw a startled look come into her eyes. Looking in the same direction, I saw a large, hand-

Fig. 208. *Little sandpipers are beautiful little mites, covered with soft down. They run very swiftly and hide most effectively.*

some gray squirrel; he would take a few, graceful bounds towards us, then stop and search about him—ever coming nearer. My sandpiper friend left her nest and ran to meet him, which she did about ten yards from her nest. Then began the prettiest bit of bird-strategy I ever seen. A bird actually wounded could not act the part any better than she did; he kept springing toward her, possibly in play, but she always avoided him and led him further away from her nest Finally she flew away to the pond leaving him in bewilderment. I do not know what he would have done, could he have caught her but I do know what would have happened if he had found her four eggs. I have seen many bird homes broken up by gray squirrels and more by the smaller red variety In order to prevent any further exploration on his part, I left the tent and chased him from the grove, an easy matter since I could shake him out of any pine he climbed

Quite often, as she sat upon the nest, she would answer the male birds as they called to one another or to their mates, from the pond It sounded alarmingly loud and clear to hear her call, at such a short distance. Just once I heard her give a low series of whistles, or rather warbles, she was probably so happy that she was singing to herself, unaware that she had an appreciative audience

Several times, the male bird came up to the edge of the clearing and conversed with her by means of low "pipings", but he never came to the nest, and I do not think he ever sat upon the eggs; at least, the bird that I saw always appeared to be the same one One morning I found only a few small pieces of egg shell Her little ones were born during the night and, somewhere in the fields, she was leading them about. The little ones are born covered with a soft gray and white down, marked with a few black stripes. They can run very fast and will hide themselves most effectively at a warning "pipe" from their mother.

Fig. 209.   NESTING-TREE OF DOWNY AND WREN.

THE WOODLAND APARTMENT.

The woodland apartment was accidentally discovered because of a feud existing between two of the families residing therein. One bright June morning I started on one of my frequent camera-hunting expeditions. my objective point being the home of a pair of Wood Thrushes that had kindly placed their nest in a very favorable position in some alders overhanging a beautiful brook. I was forcing my way slowly through a tangled mass of brakes and briers when, a short distance away. I heard the clear. ringing. rollicking song of a House Wren. It was the same wrensong with which I was familiar. full of those bubbling. gurgling tones. but 't stopped abruptly in the middle. In a few moments it sounded again and again the song was

Figs. 210-211. *The wren would alight on the stump and commence to sing; Downy would promptly drive him off.*

Fig. 212.   NEST OF DOWNY.

Opening made to show the eggs.

terminated in the same way. "Well," thought I, " that is strange! What can be troubling the little fellow. I surely must look into this".

Just beyond the fringe of the woods was a fallen apple tree, its trunk lying prone upon the ground but with several

Figs. 213, 214, 215. SOME VIEWS AT THE NEST HOLE.

gaunt grayed branches pointing upward. On the tip of one of these was Sir Wren. At the very moment that I sighted him, he lifted his head, swelled his throat and the liquid notes just trickled through his vibrating mandibles; almost at the same instant a gleam of black and white flashed through the air and he dodged just in time to escape the savage rush of a Downy Woodpecker. Alighting on another stump, the wren again burst into song, only to be pursued by the Downy as before.

Downy Woodpeckers are usually peaceable birds. But one thing could cause the strange actions of this one,—a nest. Sure enough, about half way up in the larger of the

254

Fig. 216.   *The plumage of the female was rough and worn.*

erect stubs was a little round hole,—the entrance to the
Downy home. Why should the wren so persistently stay in
this dead tree when the woodpecker was striving so fiercely
to drive him away? Again the answer revealed itself; lower
down in a shorter limb was another hole,—the wren home.

Fitting a long-focus lens to the graflex I made a view of

Fig. 217. *The four little woodpeckers looked little different
from their parents.*

the wren just as he commenced his song and also one of
the woodpecker just after he had charged.

Investigation showed that Downy already had five,
glossy, white eggs reposing on the bare wood floor of his
house. The wrens probably had arrived that very morning
for they were just commencing work on their home. Considering the quiet domestic life that these woodpeckers are
wont to lead, it is little wonder that they objected to the
presence of the boisterous and inquisitive pair of wrens.
They thought, correctly, that the continual song would sure-

Fig. 218.   *The plumage of the male was always sleek.*

ly betray the hiding place of the one spot most dear to them. Downy took upon himself the task of driving away the unwelcome neighbors. His persistence was commendable but the lack of good generalship on his part, rendered his efforts futile. Instead of devoting his energies to preventing the building of their nest, he chased the male bird every time it started to sing. The little wren seemed to regard this as a sort of bird-play and, apparently, greatly enjoyed

Fig. 219.   *The adult female (on the left) about to feed one of the young.*

it; with just a short break in his song he kept dodging and flying back and forth singing louder and louder as the chase grew warmer.

Meanwhile the female wren was just as busy as she could be, carrying in small twigs, grasses and feathers; she was so very industrious that the nest was wholly completed the first day.

Angry "chucks" proceeding from under the fallen trunk soon attracted attention to another tenant in this woodland apartment. A hole in the ground at the base of the stump showed where a Chipmunk had taken refuge and his sharp, muffled voice showed that he did not approve of

Fig. 220. *The little woodpeckers were not in the least afraid.*

259

Fig. 221. *One of them was very modest and tried to back down out of sight.*

the intrusion. A closer inspection of Downy's nest brought to my attention a fourth family occupying the top flat. A small colony of wood-boring bees had taken possession of the decayed interior of the limb about two feet above the entrance to the woodpecker nest. A number of small holes furnished the doors to this apartment; from these doors, from time to time, came tiny clouds of dust resembling smoke, showing that the occupants were still at work with their excavating.

Never did apartment block have more congenial surround-

Fig. 222. *Little Downies can climb well too.*

ings, the field-lawn was gaily decked with moon-faced daisies and golden buttercups. On one side was a large swamp, its spagnum moss-covered floor studded here and there with the rosette-like pitcher plants with deep red flowers nodding on slender stalks above the half-filled leaf pitchers that lure and destroy many insects. The humming of the bees, as they bumbled about the spotted, orange cornucopias of the jewel weed, suspended from under the leaves of the rank-growing plants that fringed the swamp, made an accompaniment to the sweet songs of Wood Thrushes.

Fig. 223. MALE HOUSE WREN.

This is "Jack" as we soon got in the habit of calling him.

On the other side the hand of man manifested itself in two shining ribbons of steel, stretching away into the distance along which thundered the sixty-mile-an-hour express and the slow, lumbering freights. not near enough to the apartment to be objectionable but just right to break the monotony of song and trees and flowers.

Fig. 224.   JACK BRINGS A SPIDER.

Ten days later the wren nest contained seven finely speckled treasures and the pair of woodpeckers were very busy trying to satisfy the unending appetites of five little woodpeckers. Both male and female Downy would enter and leave the nest without regard to us, even though we were nearly within arm's reach of them. Consequently we had no difficulty in securing a large series of photo-

Fig. 225. *Her plumage was not as smooth as Jack's,—perhaps because she worked harder.*

graphs. Downy's plumage was always clean and neat but that of his mate was quite worn and soiled, probably because she had been obliged to do nearly all of the work before the appearance of their little ones.

The adults made alternate trips with food about every five minutes, one often remaining in the nest until the other arrived. Usually they brought but a single grub at a time, but occasionally one of them would make a "lucky strike" and bring a whole mouthful. This nest was visited nearly every morning in order to keep tabs on the growth of the youngsters; the older they got, the noiser they were, making loud whining sounds when they were being fed.

One morning I found one of them clinging to the outside of the trunk and the rest crowded about the small entrance.

Fig. 226. *Jack brought a wasp,—minus wings and legs.*

They were tired of their cramped quarters and were about to explore the outside world. As we approached, they all scrambled out and commenced climbing up the trunk. We brought them down to a horizontal limb, but they were very restless; they had an idea that they were large enough to fly and wanted to try it right away. Two of them were quite bashful; every time we tried to focus the camera on them they would slide down the back side of the limb to get out of the view.

Fig. 227.

Finally, as my father was trying to straighten them out, they all scrambled on his sleeve and, one by one, climbed to his shoulder from which elevation they made their maiden flights to the woods beyond.

Meanwhile the wren eggs had also hatched and the male bird was happier than ever. So closely did his songs follow one another that it almost seemed as though a tiny, repeating phonograph must be concealed in his throat. We had visited the woodland apartment so frequently that neither of the wrens paid any attention to us. In fact we had come to know them as Jack and Jenny respectively. Like that of the male woodpecker, Jack's plumage was always sleek and orderly; also similarly and for the same reasons, that of his mate was worn, one tail feather was gone and another shorter than it ought to have been. We made pictures of

Fig. 228, 229. *Jack assumed various poses.*

them in all positions, head down, head up, bringing loads of plant lice, spiders, wasps, small grasshoppers and many other kinds of insects.

Jack devoted so much of his time to singing that his mate brought fully twice as many loads of food as he did. It was really amusing to see him sometimes try to sing when he had his beak filled to overflowing with insects; he could get in all the gurgling notes but he had to omit many of those that called for a rapid motion of the bills.

As in the case with the woodpecker, we happened to visit them on the morning the little wrens were to say goodbye to their home, but the results we obtained were entirely different. As soon as I touched the stump it seemed as though I had pulled the trigger of a gun, for the stump immediately belched forth little wrens. I clapped my hand over the opening but they poured out through my fingers and seven of the little fellows went scuttling away through the grass as fast as their wings and legs could carry them. Try as we would, we could not get more than four of them at a time and we could not persuade even one of those to sit still and look respectable while we made a portrait of him.

Fig. 230. YOUNG HOUSE WRENS.

We did not disturb the remaining tenant and I am sure that the chipmunks were delighted to see us take our final departure. They probably also was glad to see the birds go for they were not on friendly terms with one another. Chipmunks have the unfortunate habit of sometimes taking birds' eggs from their nests, a habit that forces birds to try and drive them away from the immediate vicinity of their homes. Whenever, therefore, Mr. Chipmunk appeared on the stump or tree trunk, either the Downy or wren was pretty sure to dash at him. He could easily escape the onslaughts of Downy by dodging around the limb, but the

Fig. 231. *This was an inexperienced wren; she always found it difficult to get long twigs in the small door.*

wren was even more agile than he and would put him to flight every time.

Downy did not like the colony of bees either; often I had seen him hitch around the tree trunk when they buzzed about his head. A number of times, too, I saw him spring up and catch one in his beak and carry it to his little ones. I think it quite probable that he may have exterminated the whole colony in this way before he left,—at any rate I did not notice them afterwards.

Fig. 232. AN ARTISTIC WREN HOME.

270

Fig. 233. NEST OF CAROLINA WREN.

The big Carolina Wren is not at all particular in regard to nesting site, building in hollow trees or anywhere about houses.

271

FEATHERED TYRANTS.

KINGBIRDS.

How well the name applies to these birds! Kings by
name, kings by nature and, if we may consider the concealed
orange patch on the top of their heads as a crown, kings in
raiment. Although they are usually called tyrannical and
despotic in manner, it will be noticed that they very seldom
quarrel with birds smaller than themselves, but confine their
attacks chiefly to predacious birds. By driving away
grackles, jays and squirrels, Kingbirds perform an invalua-
ble service to all their orchard friends. And their attacks
upon hawks often relieve the farmer of any anxieties in

Fig. 234. *One of their favorite lookout perches was a dried
mullein stalk.*

Fig. 235.   NEST OF KINGBIRD.

regard to his chickens. although few of the hawks touch poultry in summer.

The sight of a bird of prey is to a Kingbird, like a red flag flaunted before a bull. He immediately starts in pursuit, get above the larger bird and keeps dashing down at it. It is strange fact that hawks or crows never attempt to defend themselves but will exert themselves to the utmost to escape from the torment.

Fig. 236. *An unusual site; their nests are usually among the smaller outer branches of trees.*

Fig. 237. INSPECTION.

Although Kingbirds are commonly found about man's habitations, they have their likes and dislikes; every stranger is considered as an enemy until he has proved otherwise. The notes of Kingbirds are loud, sharp, metallic "tsee" 's, that have a disagreeable sound and carry too far for the comfort of any person who has no business in an orchard.

A pair of Kingbirds. I believe the same ones each season, returned every year to a certain orchard. As they had seen me pass through their domains so often, I thought that perhaps they might prove friendly with me and my camera, so I started to visit them one morning, armed photographic-

Fig.238.   THREE LITTLE KINGS.

ally.   As I approached the orchard they came out to meet
me, not with words of welcome, but with their usual pene-
trating notes of warning.   When I paused beneath their
nest they became so vociferous that they put the whole
orchard population into a panic; Robins, Bluebirds, Chipping and Song Sparrows, Orioles, House Wrens and a pair
of Tree Swallows, swarmed about me all giving their various notes of distress and alarm.   It required but a few
minutes of this noise to bring forth the farmer to investigate.

Fig. 239.

I first made peace with the owner of the orchard and then tried to do the same with the birds, the latter being a much more difficult matter. It required visits of an hours duration on six different days before the Kingbirds had sufficient confidence to return and feed their young while I was concealed in the tree.

Kingbird nests are quite large affairs of rootlets, grasses, gray fibres, string, paper, etc. Their four or five cream-colored eggs are very handsomely spotted with reddish-brown. Their food consists almost wholly of insects that are caught in the air. The birds have their favorite lookout perches and, so keen is their sight, that they will note passing insects at a distance of fifty yards and dash out to seize them,—a loud snapping of the mandibles testifying to their success and of the demise of another insect.

Many winged insects enter into their bill-of-fare. Large grasshoppers, dragonflies, cicadas, etc., are favorites and are even fed to the little kingbirds while in the nest.

Figs. 240, 241 *She fed them spiders, millers, small wasps, dragon-flies, etc.*

ARKANSAS KINGBIRD.

The Western or Arkansas Kingbird is a very different bird from our eastern one in appearance. Its underparts, instead of being white, are yellowish and the back is gray instead of being slate-colored. This species is common west of the Mississippi River to the Pacific Ocean. Neither their natures nor their nesting habits differ materially from those of our common bird. The one shown in the illustration chose an eave-through in which to place her home; it certainly was on a secure foundation but she failed to reckon on the sun that was to shine on the nest for about eight

278

Fig. 242. She fed and then stayed with them awhile, "zipping" loudly at the camera.

Fig. 243. *Too big for the nest, they clambered out on the limbs.*

hours of every pleasant day. She had to pay dearly for her lack of foresight, by standing over and shading her little ones during the greater part of each day.

Other Kingbirds, both the common and the western varieties, have been known to make their homes in bushes, on the tops of fence posts and even among the large branches that form the bulk of Osprey nests.

Rocky Mountain Jay.

This is a sub-species of, and quite similar in appearance to, the Canada Jay commonly found in the northern tier of states and in Canada. No bird is better known to the lumbermen, trappers and hunters along our northern borders than the Canada Jay. It is seldom, however, that it is known by this name.—being called locally "Moose Bird," "Camp-robber," "Whiskey Jack" (a corruption of the Indian name "Wis-ka-tjon"). and many others usually indicative of some of their bad traits.

Fig. 244. ARKANSAS KINGBIRD.

A handsome western species,—gray above and pale yellow below.

Fig 245. ROCKY MOUNTAIN JAY

The habits of these birds are very similar to those of our Blue Jay but they are ever so much bolder. in fact they seem to be devoid of fear for man. During the summer months they are very. very destructive to small bird life; a single pair has been known to devour the young from four Junco nests in a single day.

Fig. 245. *This jay is one of the boldest, most inquisitive and most destructive birds known.*

Their habits and their familiarity with mankind can be judged from the following from "The American Field." Anyone familiar with Canada Jays can vouch for its truth. "He will eat anything from soap to plug tobacco. His appetite and capacity to store away food is beyond belief. One day we had a dozen large salmon trout hung up to dry, but being absent from camp for a few hours we returned to find four Whiskey Jacks had totally annihilated our fish. They would fly off with pieces half a large as themselves and in a few minutes return for more I have fed them small bits until they could hardly fly enough to get to a tree. Our pork, soap tobacco and other provisions were unsafe in their sight and reach. Our Indians used to say: 'Him eat moccasins. fur cap. matches, anytink'."

In regard to the white-headed Rocky Mountain Jay, Mr. Frank M. Drew says: "In autumn, when on his first tour of inspection about the house, he hops along in a curious sidelong manner, just like a schoolgirl in a slow hurry. White-headed, grave and sedate, he seems a very paragon of propriety, and if you appear to be a suitable personage, he will be apt to give you a bit of advice Becoming confidential, he sputters out a lot of nonsense in a manner which causes you to think him a veritable 'Whiskey Jack;' yet when he is so disposed. a more bland, mind-his-own-business appearing bird will be hard to find, as will also be many small articles around camp after one of his visits, for his whimsical brain has a great fancy for anything which may be valuable to you but perfectly useless to him."

While everyone admits the great havoc wrought by these jays, their very impudence, boldness and audacity are so interesting and often amusing that nobody has the desire to kill them.

Fig. 246. NEST OF LOGGERHEAD SHRIKE

Six grayish-white eggs, spotted with yellowish-brown.

285

LOGGERHEAD SHRIKE

I. E. Hess.

Perched on the topmost twig of an osage-orange tree, his gray suit and rounded form silouetted against the leaden March sky, we see the first Loggerhead of the season. He is one of the earlier spring arrivals, being preceded only by the Robin, Bluebird, Grackle and Song Sparrow.

Totally ignoring the bleak north winds, and the gloomy

Fig. 247.   ADULT SHRIKE ON NEST.

Fig. 248. *The male brings a small caterpillar to the newly-hatched young.*

Fig. 249. *The male often stood on guard while his mate was on the nest.*

threatening clouds, he sounds his call notes merrily. This is his early spring song and how different it is from his harsh and discordant notes of the previous autumn. His bell-like calls are now far from unpleasant to our ears and we rejoice in the vocal improvement he has made.

The Northern Shrike, cousin "borealis," is an accomplished songster,—a veritable mocking bird of the northland and although we conceded him the palm upon the first hearing, we are none the less proud of our own Loggerhead for the two clear, sweet notes he is capable of producing. The Loggerhead arrives about the middle of March, the males preceding the females by but a few days.

Fig. 250. *Almost old enough to leave home.*

When Mrs Loggerhead arrives no time is lost in commencing a new home, which is usually near where last year's domicile was located. Great energy is at first displayed, but later considerable dallying is noticed and often two or three weeks are required in which to complete the new home. It is a worthy structure, however, in its finished state, and, like the scriptural house that was founded on a rock, is able to withstand the March winds that come and the April floods that are sure to descend upon it The foundation is of sticks and thorny twigs, laced and interlaced with rootlets, grasses and strings The deep and beautifully rounded inner-nest is thickly and softly lined with the fur of small animals and with feathers The waving feathers give it an appearance of warmth and comfort and it certainly proves an attractive and well-loved place, for its owners are seldom found at any distance from it.

A ride along our country roads during the first week in April will disclose many shrike nests in the process of construction. They are easily observed at this season, for it is a full month before the leafing of the hedges, and this renders them very conspicuous. This fact is in marked contrast with the nesting habits of birds in general, the great majority of which depend upon the dense foliage to hide their treasures from curious eyes Except in occasional instances, however, the conspicuity of shrike nests, does not prove detrimental to their safety, for only by extremely hard labor and an absolute indifference to thorns, can one and its contents be examined. The nests are placed in the thorniest and most impenetrable parts of the hedge-rows and usually just out of reach from the ground

From the observations of several years during which hundreds of shrike nests have been examined, I would estimate that a line drawn horizontally seven feet six inches from the ground, would pass through a majority of them, while

Fig. 251, *Bright-eyed little Shrikes,—fearless of man.*

perhaps ninety per cent. would be included between two parallel lines six and eight feet respectively above ground. This is certainly a noteworthy characteristic of his habits and represents the acumen of generations of shrike experience

A foot or more higher and the cosily-lined home would be buffeted about by the fierce spring winds, perhaps with disastrous results A foot or so lower would bring them within the limits of the curiosity and mercy of the country lad, the former trait of whom is unlimited and the latter seldom demonstrated Even located as they are we too often see a nest turned on its side, with a cornstalk thrust through it and the contents broken upon the ground Short legs and shorter arms not being able to secure, the selfishness of human nature shows itself in destroying that which cannot be obtained

Our Loggerhead is not however. discouraged by occasional reverses but will immediately proceed to build a new home and a fortnight later be happily engrossed in his new possessions It is here that we see him at his best, for he is strictly a home bird. and will not object to a much closer inspection of his life than is allowed by most birds

His personal appearance is one of meekness and does not in the least betray that cruel hidden nature that often shows itself in an undeniable manner. While Mother Nature decreed that he should prey upon the field mice and other destructive rodents. and gave to him a hooked beak that he might more readily devour his prey. we find it hard to forgive his cannibalistic tendencies when we discover a little song bird impaled upon the cruel thorns We are more willing however. to forgive his faults when we see the love and attention he bestowes upon his little mate and the unselfish care he devotes to his family of little ones.

The male proves an admirable character in his home life. He helps to build the nest and is the constant companion

of his mate during incubation. He brings her food while
she is setting or temporarily relieves her of the task. He
helps in feeding and caring for the young and, taken al-
together, is a model and exemplary husband whose virtues
far outweigh his faults. The number of eggs deposited
and making a complete set is usually six, although sometimes but five are laid.

Fig. 252. *The Flicker takes one glance about her, then dash-
es out at full speed.*

Fig. 253. NEST OF FLICKER.

Stump broken away so as to show the eggs

Fig. 254. FLICKER AT NEST-HOLE.

THE WOOD-HEWERS.

FLICKER OR GOLDEN-WINGED WOODPECKER.

All woodpeckers may be classed as carpenters; they all build their homes in the trunks or branches of trees. Usu ally decayed limbs are chosen but sometimes the larger and stronger species bore into the living wood The entrances or doors, to these homes are made circular, and just large enough to allow the birds body to slip through. The cavity within is larger and varies in depth from six inches, which is large enough for the little black and white Downy, to a foot for the Flicker and two feet or more for larger wood-peckers like the Pileated.

Just as different human beings differ in temperament. so do birds Some are very cautious especially in all their acts about their homes while others are "happy-go-lucky" and give no thought to danger. A pair of Flickers, that decided to make their home in a large chestnut tree, were of this latter class.

One morning I heard a steady, muffled chopping as I was walking along the edge of the woods Following the sound, brought me to the foot of this tree. Although it was evident that the bird was pounding away on the inside, it would have been difficult to have located the nest but for the fact that on one side of the tree, the ground was conspic-uously covered with chips. Looking upwards from this spot I could see about two inches of the tail of a busy Flicker, protruding from a hole about twenty feet up. Soon she stopped hammering, backed out and more chips came fluttering down

Both Flickers worked on this excavating for about a week before the chamber was large enough to suit them; they both had the same careless habit of simply dropping the chips from the opening. It was an advertisement notifying beast, bird or man that above was the nest of some wood-peckers Of course these tell-tale chips may have had nothing to do with the outcome, but one day, soon after their set of eggs was completed, I saw a pair of red squirrels playing about the tree and often going into the Flicker nest. An investigation showed that the eggs were missing.

More careful were the Flickers that dwelt in a large willow overhanging a swiftly flowing brook. Every chip was

Fig. 255. *Young flickers do not like to pose before a camera.*

prudently carried away for a distance of a hundred yards or more before it was dropped.

Flickers are very different in their habits from other woodpeckers. They get more of their food from the ground than they do from trees; they are exceedingly fond of ants, one bird often destroying a whole colony at one meal. They also usually alight on branches crosswise, as a perching bird does, instead of lengthwise like the other members of the family.

Five to eight glossy white eggs are laid, directly upon the bare floor of the house or what few chips happen to remain. For the first week of their lives, little Flickers are fed by regurgitation, that is, food that has been partly digested by the parent. During the remainder of their stay in the nest, the little birds are fed largely upon ants, spiders and small worms or caterpillars. They are very noisy when they are nearly fledged. and their clamor is appalling when their frequent meals come around

I have never been able to make little Flickers pose before the camera so as to secure a respectable picture. They always get into the most awkward and uncomfortable positions, and bite and claw one another so that it is almost impossible to keep any kind of order. Judging from the squealing and confusion that always greets the return of one of their parents to the nest. I doubt if the old birds can make their youngsters behave much better than I have been able to.

Red-headed Woodpecker.

This species is one of the most beautiful of woodpeckers. The black, the white, and the red are distributed in such large, clear-cut areas that the bird cannot escape unnoticed when at rest or in flight. As a rule, I believe that birds of this species are rather proud and wish to attract as much attention as possible. They have loud, whining voices and, especially during the mating and early nesting season, seem to try to make all the noise they possibly can.

In many respects, "Red-heads" are just the opposite of Flickers. Flickers are peaceable birds,—never known to start a neighborhood quarrel; but Red-headed Woodpeckers are "bird-brawlers,"—never so happy as when engaged in arguments, or even rough and tumble fights with some neighbor. I am sorry to have to admit, too, that their adversaries are seldom guilty of any offense but usually have to protect themselves against the depredations of the Red-heads

298

Fig. 256.   YOUNG RED-HEADED WOODPECKER.

The head and back is gray instead of red and black respectively as in the adults.

I have often seen the results of atrocious acts committed by these birds, in the shape of devastated homes of other birds, and once I saw a pair of them perform the act. It was in an old Virginia swamp where many tall, whitened, naked tree trunks were still standing. Two pairs of the woodpeckers were in evidence; I had found the nest of one of them, about twenty feet above ground in one of these dead trees.

Many Brown-headed Nuthatches were also nesting there, and I had located one of their nests,—high up. where I could not get to it. They were very busy carrying food to little birds, through the little round hole in the trunk that led to their dwelling. One day as I was about fifty yards away from this tree, I saw one pair of the Red-heads sweep by with their usual undulating flight and alight beside the Nuthatch home. Evidently the cavity was shallow, for each woodpecker, in turn, reached his head in and pulled out a squirming little nuthatch. The female bore her prize away to her own nest, but the male took his to a near tree, pulled it to pieces and ate it himself.

Of course it is but for a short season that these woodpeckers are destructive to the young and eggs of other birds. During the rest of the year they are useful in destroying a great many wood-borers. larvae, etc. They have the habit, shared by many birds that migrate little if at all, of storing up supplies of food for future use. They often conceal nuts in crevices in bark or in holes that they may make for that purpose. Of course some other bird has just as good a chance of eating the hoard as the one that stored it, but he, on the other hand. also uses goods stored by other individuals

Yellow-bellied Sapsucker.

Here we have another type of woodpecker. The Flicker has a sticky tongue. perfectly adapted for catching the ants it likes so well. The Red-headed Woodpecker has a tongue,

Fig. 257. *Adult Red-headed Woodpecker at the entrance to her nest.*

Fig 258   ADULT SAPSUCKER

the tip of which is armed with tiny barbs, adapted to spear-
ing insects and drawing them from under the bark or wood
of trees   The tongue of a Sapsucker is covered with fine
hairs at the tip making a small brush with which he can lap
up the sap that oozes from holes he bores through the bark
of trees.

His food does not, however, consist even largely of sap,
for he catches probably as many insects as others of the
woodpecker family   Sapsuckers very frequently come to
the suet and nut banquets that are spread for winter birds;
it was while partaking of such a feast that the pictures of
the Sapsuckers shown here were secured

Fig. 259. YOUNG SAPSUCKER.

You can see the many holes he has bored through the bark so as to get the sap that collects.

303

Fig. 260. ENGLISH SPARROWS

Pests, even worse than the Brown-tailand Gypsy Moths that are devastating New England shade trees. Were it not for these sparrows, useful birds would come into the cities and detroy these moths.

HOW BIRD PHOTOGRAPHS ARE MADE

EQUIPMENT.—Nearly everyone uses a camera of some sort, but every camera is not suitable for our purpose of bird photography. Plate cameras are used almost exclusively, not because plates are better than films, but chiefly because with those using films you cannot focus the picture you wish to secure on a ground glass and because they are not built with sufficiently long bellows.

More than three-quarters of the pictures shown in this book were taken at distances between three and four feet; working at this distance it is absolutely necessary that a very sharp focus be secured; this must be done, not by guesswork, but by careful viewing the image on the ground glass. I know of no successful bird photographer but who uses a plate camera for most of his or her work

I always advise anyone to purchase as good an outfit as they can afford. Undoubtedly the very best outfit that can be secured is the 4 x 5 revolving-back Graflex fitted with a seven and one-half inch convertible anastigmat lens in a compound shutter. Unfortunately, however, such an outfit is very expensive. Personally, if I could have but one camera,—one that I could carry about with me comfortably and use for all purposes I should select a 4 x 5 plate camera having a bellows capacity of at least twelve inches and fitted with a seven inch anastigmat lens in a compound shutter This outfit would cost in the neighborhood of seventy-five dollars, but would be capable of the most exacting work in all branches except high-speed work. When traveling, one can use a film-pack with this outfit, securing all the conveniences and compactness of a kodak, yet have the ability to do work at close range that cannot be satisfactorily done with the latter instrument.

The best is desirable but is not necessary. Very good results may be obtained with the regular 4 x 5 camera and equipment that can be purchased for twenty-five dollars

The results depend chiefly upon the person making the pictures. Let a skillful operator use the two instruments and the best pictures taken with the cheaper camera will be fully equal to the best taken with an expensive one, while the poorest taken with the latter will be just as undesirable as the poorest secured with the cheap outfit; but the average of those taken with a high grade lens will probably be considerably better than those taken with an ordinary one.

Nearly every bird picture is made with the camera on a tripod. For a light camera. I prefer a telescopic metal tripod as they are very compact and rigid.

One of the chief requisites of bird photographs, or of any other subject, is that the principal objects and foreground be absolutely sharp. Nests and nesting sites are always photographed with a small stop or aperture to the lens giving an exposure adapted to the quality and intensity of the light.

A small ball and socket joint that can be procured from your supply dealer for about a dollar, will allow you to point the camera downward at a sharp angle so as to conveniently photograph nests located on or near the ground. Care and judgment must be used in removing or tying out of the way any branches, leaves or grasses that come between the camera and nest and appear out of focus on the ground glass.

The very best photographic results can be obtained on bright cloudy days. Bright sun shining on a nest makes too strong a contrast of light and shadow for pleasing effects, such light should be screened, perferably with a white cloth. Do not destroy any of the foliage that is necessary to shelter the nest from sun rain or observation; objectionable leaves may be very easily tied with thread so as to be out of the way.

Photographing Young Birds

Beautiful pictures of very young birds in the nest may

often be secured by focusing very carefully on the nest then slightly jarring their home. Thinking that their parents are returning with food. often the tiny heads, with wide-open mouths. will be raised expectantly. Such pictures, of course, have to be made with the lens wide open and with a speed of not less than one-hundredth of a second. Little birds should not be taken from the nest for any purpose until they are fully feathered. If they are not large and strong enough to perch on a branch it is folly to try and take them in that position. for the result will be unnatural, forced and ugly.

Families of little birds, side by side. on twigs make excellent bird studies and are easily taken. The branch should be selected and your camera set in position and carefully focussed before disturbing the birds. In such cases the lens is always used at its largest aperture for depth of focus is not only not wanted but is undesirable. A softly blended background of as nearly a uniform shade as can be produced is the effect to aim for. Handle the little birds as gently as possible and try and get them to pose easily and gracefully on that section of the branch that is shown on the ground glass. Avoid any quick motions for, should one of the little fellows be startled and try to fly, you will find it very difficult to induce him to remain where you want him to afterwards

PHOTOGRAPHING ADULT BIRDS

Armed with a reflecting camera it is not difficult to secure pictures of many of the larger birds, such as gulls. terns, ospreys, etc, in flight. One may even occasionally get near enough to take a passably good picture of some of the smaller birds. If, however, anyone depended upon rambling through the fields and woods trying to get these "lucky shots," the photographs representing his season's work would be few in number and of comparatively little value.

Lenses are mechanical implements. A lens of a certain

focal length will always make the same sized image of a certain sized bird at the same distance. Unfortunately this image of the smaller birds is very tiny unless the camera is very close to the subject. How then, can we get close enough to the birds or get them to come close enough to us? Certainly not by chasing them. The devotion of birds to their offspring is not surpassed by that of human mothers for their children; for them, they will face any danger. Here then, is the magnet that will unfailingly draw the bird within reaching distance of the camera-eye.

Having located a nest in a get-at-able position, there are two practical methods of procedure in order to get the desired pictures. I will first mention the tent method as that is much the best. Birds pay little or no attention to inanimate objects, a fact which makes bird photography possible. I believe it was Kearton in England, who first conceived this idea of photographing from a blind. He used an artificial tree trunk that he set in place near birds' nests and from the inside of which he made his pictures. It has been found that it is not even necessary that the blind bear resemblance to surrounding objects.

The simplest, most compact and most portable form of tent is that known as the umbrella-tent. An ordinary, strong umbrella is fitted with extensions so that the handle may be lengthened to about six feet; a covering is made to fit over the top and droop to the ground. This simple tent can be held rigidly upright by three guy cords from the top.

The tent can be used successfully from which to photograph birds returning to their eggs, but only when the latter are in advanced stages of incubation, at which time home ties will be strong enough to induce the bird to return. Too early an attempt at its use will cause the bird to desert its nest

The following will represent the mode of procedure in nearly every instance where a nest is not more than six feet above ground Consider that we have found the nest of a Chestnut-sided Warbler in a favorable position and that the young are about a week old. We arrive with our out-fit at a time of day when the light is most favorable. The tent is quickly placed in position so that its nearest side is but three feet from the nest; in this side we have a series of flaps the proper one of which is pinned back so that the camera can be focussed on the subject We study the image on the ground glass, tying back foliage that causes blurs in the foreground. A single branch shades the nest from the sun; a black thread is tied to this, carried around a branch on a neighboring bush and then to the tent A gen-tle pull on this thread elevates the shade-branch so as to leave the entire nest strongly illuminated whenever we desire.

Five minutes from the time we arrived, we have every-thing in readiness and are standing or sitting within our shelter If everything goes well, within ten minutes we will probably see the warblers coming and going, feeding their little ones just as though we were not there. We usually allow them to make two or three visits before making ex-posures as the click of the shutter often startles them the first time they hear it With care, plate after plate may be exposed without alarming the adult birds in the least Just imagine it! Free wild birds performing their household duties within arm's reach of you and apparently not aware of your presence. That sounds easy, doesn't it? It is easy, too if everything turns out as we want it to. Unfortu nately, however, birds have a way of upsetting our plans, so that try as we will, we may fail to get even a single picture

The tent allows of accurate observations of events at the nest and also of perfect control of the camera Often, however, the use of a tent may not be feasible; the nest may be too high or circumstances may prevent your having or procuring a satisfactory tent, yet good pictures can almost as readily be obtained. The only difference is that the camera must be operated from a distance, which of course, necessitates going to it to change plates between exposures. Sometimes the shutter is operated by a long tube leading from your place of concealment, but the better way is to use a black linen thread. With the thread you can operate from a greater distance if necessary and you can be certain that an exposure is made when you pull it. To release the shutter by this method I attach a rubber band to camera bed and pass it over the release lever which is held in place by a splinter of wood of correct length between it and the camera bed. The thread is attached near one end of this bit of wood so that a slight pull will bring it from under the lever and the elastic band will complete the work.

Obviously no rules can be given for the very many different problems that are offered by different nests; they have to be solved by the photographer and it is his ability or inability to cope with adverse condition that will mark him as a successful or an unsuccessful bird photographer. The camera may have to be lashed up in trees; sunlight may have to be reflected on the nest by a mirror; but whatever you have to do, always bear in mind that the safety of the young birds is of much greater importance than the securing of a picture. Some photographers drape their tent with leafy branches so as to make it less conspicuous; you can suit your own fancy in regard to that, as the birds do not care whether it is draped or not. If a tent is not used, the camera should be covered with a black focussing cloth so as to prevent fogging of the plate by chance leakage of light.

INDEX

312

Lightning Source UK Ltd.
Milton Keynes UK
23 November 2010

163313UK00007B/11/P